RECORDS OF THE PAST

BEING ENGLISH TRANSLATIONS

OF THE

ANCIENT MONUMENTS OF EGYPT AND WESTERN ASIA

NEW SERIES

EDITED BY A. H. SAYCE.

VOL. I

This is volume one of the second series of *Records of the Past*, under the editorship of A. H. Sayce. This volume includes two versions of the Creation epic, today known as the *Enuma Elish*, and several historical texts, including the Babylonian Chronicles, and the hair-raising *Inscription of Tiglath-Pileser I*.

PREFACE

THE favourable reception accorded to the first series of *Records of the Past*, and the hope more than once expressed since its discontinuance that a similar series would be again started, have led to this second attempt to lay before the public some of the most important documents left us by the civilised nations of the ancient Oriental world. During the ten years that have elapsed since the first series was concluded, Assyrian research may be said to have entered upon a new phase. Expeditions have returned from Babylonia, bringing with them the spoils of ancient libraries, the clay tablets preserved in the British Museum and elsewhere have been copied and examined with increased industry and exactness, and students have been flocking to the new study in Germany and America. The decipherment of the cuneiform inscriptions of Van has opened up a fresh world of language and history, and the geography of Western Asia in the Assyrian epoch has been mapped out in almost all its essential details.

The increase of materials, and more especially of labourers in the field of research, has made our knowledge of the Assyrian lexicon at once wider and more accurate. Inscriptions which were still obscure ten years ago can now be read with a fair approach to exactness, while many of the translations proposed in the former series of the *Records* can be amended in many respects. Indeed there are certain cases in which the progress of knowledge has shown the tentative renderings of a few years ago to be so faulty, if not misleading, that it has been determined to replace them by revised translations in the series which is now being issued.

The new series will, it is hoped, be found to be an improvement upon its predecessor in certain points. The translations will be provided with fuller introductions and notes, bearing more particularly upon the history, geography, and theology of the texts, and drawing attention to the illustrations they afford of the Scriptures of the Old Testament. The historical inscriptions, moreover, will be published, so far as is possible, in chronological order.

In one point, however, a difference will be noticed between the plan of this second series of *Records* and that of the first. The value of a translation from a language known only to a few scholars depends in large measure upon the confidence with which its precise wording can be accepted. The writer who wishes to make use of a translation from an Egyptian or Assyrian text for historical or controversial purposes ought to know where it is certain, and where it is only possible, or at most probable. He ought to receive warning of passages or words or readings of doubtful character, and the translator ought to provide proofs of any new renderings he may give. In the present series of volumes, accordingly, doubtful words and expressions will be followed by a note of interrogation, the preceding word being put into italics where necessary: otherwise italics will be used only for the transliteration of proper names or words which cannot at present be translated. The notes will contain a justification of new translations, whether of words hitherto undeciphered or of words to which a different signification has hitherto been attached. The names of individuals will be distinguished from those of deities or localities by being printed in Roman type, whereas the names of deities and localities will be in capitals.

Though exploration and discovery have been carried on actively in Egypt during the last decade, thanks mainly to the Egypt Exploration Fund and the enterprise of Professor Maspero, the results have not been so startling or numerous as those which have attended the progress of the younger study of Assyriology. There is not the same reason for amending the translations, previously published, of Egyptian documents, nor has any large number of historical texts been brought to light. Instead, therefore, of publishing alternately translations from the Assyrian and Egyptian monuments, Assyrian and Egyptian texts will appear in the same volume, though it will doubtless happen that the Assyrian element will preponderate in some volumes, the Egyptian element in others. Egyptian and Assyrian, of course, will not be exclusively represented; Phœnicians and Proto-Armenians have left us written monuments, comparatively few though they may be, and the *Records of the Past* would be incomplete without such important inscriptions as that of the Moabite king Mesha or of the Hebrew Pool of Siloam.

In commending the first volume of this new series of *Records* to the approval of the public, the Editor must not forget to say that the enterprise is international, eminent scholars belonging to all nationalities having consented to take part in it, and that if his name appears somewhat too frequently in the present volume, it is a fault which shall not occur again.

A. H. SAYCE.

QUEEN'S COLLEGE, OXFORD,

3 *d August* 1888.

EQUIVALENTS OF THE HEBREW LETTERS IN THE TRANSLITERATION OF ASSYRIAN NAMES MENTIONED IN THESE VOLUMES.

א	*a, '*	ל	*l*
ב	*b*	מ	*m*
ג	*g*	נ	*n*
ד	*d*	ס	*'s, s*
ה	*h*	ע	*e*
ו	*u, v*	פ	*p*
ז	*z*	צ	*ts*
ח	*kh*	ק	*q*
ת	*dh*	ר	*r*
י	*i, y*	ש	*s, sh*
כ	*k*	ט	*t*

N.B.—Those Assyriologists who transcribe ש by *sh* use *s* for ס. The Assyrian *e* represents a diphthong as well as ע.

In the Introductions and Notes W.A.I. denotes *The Cuneiform Inscriptions of Western Asia*, in five volumes, published by the Trustees of the British Museum.

The Assyrian Calendar

	CORRESPONDING MONTHS
1. Ni'sannu (Nisan).	March—April.
2. Aaru (Iyyar).	April—May.
3. 'Sivanu (Sivan)	May—June.
4. Dûzu (Tammuz)	June—July.
5. Abu (Ab)	July—August.

6. Ululu (Elul)   August—September.
7. Tasritu (Tisri)   September—October.
8. Arakh-savna (Marchesvan) "the 8th month" October—November.
9. Ki'silivu (Chisleu).   November—December.
10. Dhabitu (Tebet)   December—January.
11. Sabadhu (Sebat)   January—February.
12. Addaru (Adar)   February—March.
13. Arakh-makhru (Ve-Adar), the intercalary month.

THE DYNASTIC TABLETS AND CHRONICLES OF THE BABYLONIANS

BY THE EDITOR

CHRONOLOGY is the skeleton of history, and until we can find the correct chronological place for a historical monument it loses a large part of its value. Thanks to the lists of the so-called eponyms, by means of whom the Assyrians dated their years, the chronology of the Assyrian kings has long since been placed upon a satisfactory footing as far back as the tenth century before our era. The dates, moreover, assigned by Sennacherib to Tiglath-Pileser I. (B.C. 1106), and Tukulti-Uras, the son of Shalmaneser I. (B.C. 1290), as well as the lengthy genealogies with which these kings are connected, enable us to extend Assyrian chronology back for another five hundred years, though, of course, with only approximate accuracy.

While our knowledge of Assyrian chronology, however, has thus been tolerably fixed for a long time past, we have had to depend upon the vague and contradictory statements of Greek writers for our knowledge of the chronology of the older kingdom of Babylonia. Apart from the invaluable table of kings known as Ptolemy's Canon, which belongs to the later period of Babylonian history, and the unsatisfactory list of dynasties excerpted from an epitomist of Bêrôssos, our only monumental authorities for Babylonian chronology were the Assyrian inscriptions themselves, together with a few fragments of a dynastic tablet brought to light by Mr. George Smith and the so-called Synchronous History of Assyria and Babylonia, of which I published a translation in the former series of *Records of the Past* (vol. iii.) This "Synchronous History" was composed by an Assyrian scribe, and consists of brief notices of the occasions on which the kings of the two countries had entered into relation, hostile or otherwise, with one another. Since my translation was published in 1874, another large fragment of the tablet has been discovered, and accordingly I purpose giving a new translation of the whole document in a future volume of the present series. The "Synchronous History" gives no dates, and consequently its chronological value depends upon our knowledge of the respective dates to which the Assyrian monarchs mentioned in it belong.

Within the last few years a number of discoveries due to Mr. Pinches has entirely changed our position in regard to the chronology of the Babylonian kings. As I have already stated, Mr. Smith found among the tablets brought from the royal library of Nineveh a small fragment which, as he perceived, contained the names and regnal years of the kings of Babylonia, arranged in dynasties. The work to which it belonged must accordingly have been similar to that from which Berossos derived his dynastic list of Chaldean monarchs. Mr. Smith published the fragment, with a translation and commentary, in the *Transactions of the Society of Biblical Archæology*, iii. 2 (1874). It is written on both sides, and the tablet once consisted of six columns, each containing about seventy lines. I will call it the "Third Dynastic Tablet."

The next discovery was made by Mr. Pinches six years later among the inscriptions brought from the site of Babylon by the overseer of Mr. Hormuzd Rassam. He found among them a small tablet of unbaked clay, quite complete and inscribed on both sides. It contains the names of the kings belonging to two early dynasties, the number of years reigned by each king being added to the names in the case of the first dynasty. The tablet seems to be a sort of schoolboy's exercise, having been copied from some larger work in order to be committed to memory. The Reverse has been published by Mr. Pinches in the *Proceedings of the Society of Biblical Archaeology*, 7th December 1880, and I will call it the "First Dynastic Tablet."

Another and more important document—the "Second Dynastic Tablet"—was published by Mr. Pinches, with a translation and explanation, in the *Proceedings of the Society of Biblical Archæology*, 6th May 1884. This is also a tablet of unbaked clay from Babylonia, and it contains a list of the Babylonian sovereigns, arranged in dynasties, from the first dynasty which made the city of Babylon the capital down to the period of the Persian conquest. The number of regnal years is added to the name of each king and the length of time each dynasty lasted is duly recorded. The names of some of the kings are written in an abbreviated form: this is especially the case with those belonging to the second dynasty.

The list, it will be observed, is confined to the dynasties which reigned in Babylon itself. No notice is taken of the kings and dynasties who ruled in "Accad and Sumer" before Babylon became the capital of the empire. The lost columns of the "Third Dynastic Tablet" show how numerous they were, and the fact is borne out by the bricks and other monuments of early Chaldean monarchs whose names do not occur among the successors of 'Sumu-abi. Most of the kings, indeed, whose names are known to us in connection with the temples they built or restored belonged to older dynasties than those which had their seat in the city of Babylon.

A considerable number of their names is to be found in another tablet brought by Mr. Rassam from Assyria, and published by Mr. Pinches in the *Proceedings of the Society of Biblical Archæology*, 11th January 1881. A small portion of it had already been published in W.A.I., ii. 65, and had given rise to a good many false conclusions. The object of this tablet was philological and not chronological; in fact the writer expressly states that the names of the kings were "not written according to their chronological order." He merely wished to furnish the Semitic or Assyro-Babylonian translations of the Accado-Sumerian and Kassite names borne by so many of the early princes, and in some cases of the mode in which the names of Semitic kings were pronounced or written by their Accadian subjects.

Among the latter is the name of Sargon of Accad, the ancient hero of the Semitic population of Chaldæa, who founded the first Semitic empire in the country and established a great library in his capital city of Agade or Accad near Sippara. The seal of his librarian, Ibni-sarru, of very beautiful workmanship, is now in Paris, and has been published by M. de Clercq (*Collection de Clercq*, pl. 5, No. 46), while a copy of his annals, together with those of his son Naram-Sin, is to be found in W.A.I., iv. 34. His date has been fixed by a passage in a cylinder of Nabonidos discovered in the ruins of the temple of the Sun-god at Sippara, and published in W.A.I., v. 64. The antiquarian zeal of Nabonidos led him to excavate among the foundations of the temple in the hope of finding the cylinder of Naram-Sin, who was known to have been the founder of it, and he tells us (col. ii. 56 *seq.*):—

> "I sought for its old foundation-stone, and eighteen cubits deep
>
> I dug into the ground, and the foundation-stone of Naram-Sin, the son of Sargon, which for 3200 years no king who had gone before me had seen, the Sun-god, the great lord of E-Babara, the temple of the seat of the goodness of his heart, let me see, even me."

In the opinion, therefore, of Nabonidos, a king who had a passion for investigating the past records of his country, Naram-Sin reigned 3200 years before his own time, that is to say, about B.C. 3700.

Before the rise of the Semitic kingdom of Sargon of Accad, lies that earlier Accado-Sumerian period when Babylonia was still in the hands of a people who spoke an agglutinative language, such as those of the modern Turks or Finns, and had originated the cuneiform system of writing and the primitive civilisation of the Chaldean cities. Relics of this ancient period have been discovered by M. de Sarzec in the mounds of Tel-loh, and the Sumerian inscriptions which they bear are now being deciphered by French scholars, more especially by M. Amiaud. M. Amiaud has been good enough to introduce the historical documents of Babylonia and Assyria to the readers of the present series of *Records of the Past*, by his translations of these oldest memorials of human life and thought in the valley of the Euphrates. If Sargon of

Accad lived about B.C. 3800, the kings of Telloh must have flourished as far back as the fourth millennium before our era.

The last chronological document brought to light during the last few years is in many respects the most important of all. This is what has been termed "The Babylonian Chronicle" by its discoverer, Mr. Pinches, who gave an abstract of it in the *Proceedings of the Society of Biblical Archæology*, 6th May 1884. Since then, the text has been published with a translation and commentary by Dr. Winckler in the *Zeitschrift für Assyriologie*, ii. 2, 3 (1887); it has also been translated by Dr. Oppert. The tablet (which is marked 84. 2-11, 356) was brought from Babylonia and is inscribed on both sides with four columns of text. It was a copy or compilation made by a Babylonian in the reign of Darius from older records, and must have been similar to the document from which Ptolemy's Canon of Babylonian kings was extracted. Like the latter it starts from the era of Nabonassar, B.C. 747.

The chronicle is written from a Babylonian point of view, and must therefore be checked by contemporaneous Assyrian inscriptions. What they describe as Assyrian successes are sometimes passed over altogether or represented as Babylonian victories. The Assyrian kings Tiglath-Pileser III and Shalmaneser IV are not acknowledged under the names they had adopted from two of the most illustrious monarchs of the first Assyrian empire, but under their original names of Pul and Ululâ; Sargon, on the other hand, whose name was that of the favourite hero of Babylonian legend, is known by the same name in the Chronicle as he is on the monuments of Assyria. At the same time the Chronicle helps us in correcting the inaccuracies of the Assyrian accounts, where, for example, Suzub represents both Nergal-yusezib and Musezib-Merodach. In fact, it confirms the judgment, already expressed by Assyriologists, that Sennacherib is the least trustworthy of the royal historians of Assyria.

We are at present ignorant of the precise way in which the Babylonians reckoned their chronology. In Assyria the years were named after certain officers, ordinarily known as eponyms, who were changed each year, and as most of the institutions of Assyria were derived from Babylonia it is very probable that the system of counting time by the names of the eponyms was also of Babylonian invention. How far we can trust the dates assigned to the kings of the earlier dynasties is open to question. The length of reign assigned to the kings of the dynasties of the sea and of Bit-Bazi in the Second and Third Dynastic Tablets do not agree, while the number of regnal years given to the several kings of the first dynasty of Babylon not only plays on the same ciphers but is suspiciously long. On the other hand, the contract-tablets belonging to the time of Khammuragas imply that his reign was not a short one.

There is evidence in a later part of the dynastic lists that at least one name has been omitted. Dr. Winckler has published (in the *Zeitschrift für Assyriologie*, ii. 3)

the commencement of an inscription from Babylonia (marked 83.1-18) belonging to a certain king of Babylon, who calls himself Kuri-galzu the son of Kara-Urus. Dr. Winckler shows that this must be Kuri-galzu II, and that his name ought to occur in the list between those of Kara-Urus and Rimmon-nadin-suma. It is quite possible that other reigns have fallen out in other parts of the lists.

The lacuna in the Second Dynastic Tablet between the beginning of the eighth dynasty and the commencement of the reign of Nabonassar unfortunately prevents us from determining with certainty the date assigned by the compiler of it to 'Sumu-abi. But there are two synchronisms between Babylonian and Assyrian history which may serve to remedy the defect. According to Sennacherib, Merodach-nadin-akhe defeated Tiglath-Pileser I, 418 years before his own conquest of Babylon, that is to say, in B.C. 1106, while the "Synchronous History" makes Assur-bilkala, the son of Tiglath-Pileser I, the contemporary of Merodach-sapik-kullat, and Assur-dân the great-grandfather of Tiglath-Pileser I, the contemporary of Zamama-nadin-suma, the father of Assur-dân being contemporaneous with Rimmon-[suma-natsir?]. If Merodach-nadin-akhe is the ninth king of the dynasty of Isin, the date of Zamama-nadin-suma will be B.C. 1160, agreeing very well with the period to which the end of the reign of Assur-dân should be assigned. In this case Sagasalti-buryas, who flourished 800 years before Nabonidos, will not be identical with the Saga-sal[tiyas] of the dynastic list. The reign of Khammuragas will have commenced B.C. 2282, the first dynasty of Babylon establishing its power there in B.C. 2394.

We learn from the inscriptions of Khammuragas that he was the first of his dynasty to rule over the whole of Babylonia. A rival dynasty had previously reigned at Karrak in the south, while the Elamites had invaded portions of the country and probably held them in subjection. Assur-bani-pal states that the Elamite king Kudur-Nankhundi had carried away the image of the goddess Nana from Babylonia 1635 years before his own time, or about B.C. 2285, and contract-tablets refer to the conquest of "the lord of Elam and King Rim-Agu" of Karrak by Khammuragas. A large number of contract-tablets, indeed, belong not only to the reigns of Khammuragas and his son Samsu-iluna, but also to the reign of Rim-Agu, who seems to have been master of the greater part of Chaldæa before his overthrow by the king of Babylon. George Smith was probably right in identifying him with the son of the Elamite prince Kudur-Mabug, who ruled at Larsa and claimed the imperial title of "king of Sumer and Accad."

The rise of the empire of Khammuragas brought with it a revival of learning and literature such as had marked the rise of the empire of Sargon. The calendar appears to have been reformed at this period, and the great native work on astronomy and astrology put into the shape in which it has come down to us. The reign thus formed an era somewhat similar to that of Nabonassar, and it is therefore curious to see how closely the date I have assigned to it corresponds with that arrived at by von Gutschmidt from classical sources for the beginning of the Babylonian epoch. If the Latin translation can be trusted (*Simplicius ad Arist. de Cœlo,* 503 A), the astronomical observations sent by Kallisthenes from Babylon to Aristotle in B.C. 331 reached back for 1903 years (*i.e.* to B.C. 2234). Bêrôssos the Chaldean historian, according to Pliny (N.H. vii. 57), stated that these observations commenced at Babylon 490 years before the Greek era of Phoroneus, and consequently in B.C. 2243. According to Stephanos of Byzantium, Babylon was built 1002 years before the date (given by Hellanikos) for the siege of Troy (B.C. 1229), which would bring us to B.C. 2231, while Ktesias, according to George Syncellus, made the reign of Belos or Bel-Merodach last for fifty-five years from B.C. 2286 to 2231. The fifty-five years of Belos agree with the fifty-five of Khammuragas.

I add here the Canon of Babylonian kings given by Ptolemy in the Almagest.

	B.C.
1. Nabonassar (Nabu-natsir), 14 years	747
2. Nadios (Nadinu), 2 years	733
3. Khinziros and Poros (Yukin-zira and Pul), 5 years	731
4. Iloulaios or Yougaios 1 (Ululâ), 5 years	726
5. Mardokempados (Merodach-baladan), 12 years	721
6. Arkeanos (Sargon), 5 years	709
7. Interregnum for 2 years 1	704
8. Belibos (Bel-ebus), 2 3 years	702
9. Aparanadios 3 (Assur-nadin-suma), 6 years	700
10. Regebelos (Nergal-yusezib), 1 year	694
11. Mesesimordakos (Musezib-Merodach), 4 years	693
12. Interregnum for 8 years.	689
13. Asaridinos (Esar-haddon), 13 years	681
14. Saosdoukhinos (Saul-suma-yukin), 20 years	668
15. Kineladanos (Kandalanu), 22 years	648
16. Nabopolassaros (Nabu-pal-utsur), 21 years	626
17. Nabokolassaros (Nebuchadnezzar), 43 years	605
18. Ilauaroudamos (Avil-Merodach), 2 years	562
19. Nerigasolasaros (Nergal-sarra-utsur), 4 years	560 4
20. Nabonadios (Nabu-nahid), 17 years	556

Footnotes

11:1 Yougaios, if it is not due to a corruption of the text, may represent the name of Vagina, the father of Merodach-baladan.

12:1 Filled up according to Alexander Polyhistor by the brother of Sennacherib, by Hagisa or Akises for thirty days, and by Merodach-baladan for six months.

12:2 Called Elibos by Alexander Polyhistor.

12:3 Assordanios according to Alexander Polyhistor.

12:4 Josephus (from Berossos) here inserts Laborosoarkhodos, the infant son of Neriglissor, for three months.

No. I.—TRANSLATION OF THE FIRST DYNASTIC TABLET FROM BABYLON

OBVERSE

1. 'Sumu-abi, the king: 15 years.

2. 'Sumu-la-ilu, the son of the same: 35 years.

3. Zabû, the son of the same: 14 years.

4. Abil-Sin, the son of the same: 18 years.

5. Sin-muballidh, the son of the same: 30 years.

6. Khammu-ragas, ₁ the son of the same: 55 years.

7. 'Sam'su-iluna, ₂ the son of the same: 35 years.

8. Ebisum, ₃ the son of the same: 25 years.

9. Ammi-satana, the son of the same: 25 years.

10. Ammi-sadugga, ₄ the son of the same: 21 years.

11. 'Sam'su-satana (?), the son of the same: 31 years.

12. 11 kings of the dynasty of BABYLON.

1. (The dynasty of) URU-AZAGGA. ₅ Anman the king.

2. Ki-[AN] Nigas. ₆

3. Damki-ili-su. ₇

4. Is-ki-pal. ₁

5. Sussi. ₂

6. Gul-ki-sar. ₃

7. Kirgal-dara-mas, the son of the same.

8. A-dara-kalama, the son of the same. ₄

9. A-kur-du-ana. ₅

10. Melam-kurkura. ₆

11. Ea-ga(mil?). ₇

12. 1[1] kings of the dynasty of URU-AZAGGA.

Footnotes

13:1 The first five names of the dynasty are Semitic. Khammuragas is Kassite or Kossæan, and is interpreted "of a large family." Sin-muballidh may have married a foreign wife.

13:2 "The Sun-god (is) our god," another Semitic name.

13:3 "The doer," also Semitic.

13:4 Kassite, interpreted "the family is established."

13:5 Uru-azagga is now represented by a part of the mounds of Telloh (the ancient Sirpurla) or its immediate vicinity.

13:6 Nigas was an Elamite word.

13:7 Semitic, signifying "gracious is his god."

14:1 Perhaps to be read in Semitic Sapin-mat-nukurti, "the sweeper away of the land of the foe." The name seems to have been a title.

14:2 Perhaps the Semitic *sussu*, "sixty."

14:3 In Semitic Muabbid-kissati, "the destroyer of hosts."

14:4 Apparently, therefore, the son of the preceding king.

14:5 Rendered by the Semitic Abil-Bel-u'sum-same, "the son of Bel (the lord) of the treasury of heaven."

14:6 "The glory of the world."

14:7 The last character is partially destroyed. If my restoration is correct, the name would be Semitic and signify "Ea has rewarded."

No. 2.—TRANSLATION OF THE SECOND DYNASTIC TABLET FROM BABYLON

COLUMN I

The first eleven lines are destroyed.

12. 11 kings [of the dynasty of BABYLON] for [294 years].

———————

13. Anma[n] for [5]1 (years).

14. KI-AN [Nigas] for 55 (years).

15. Damki-ili[su] for 46 1 (years).

16. Is-ki-[pal] for 15 (years).

17. Sussi, (his) brother, for 27 (years).

18. Gul-ki-[sar] for 55 (years).

19. Kirgal-[dara-mas] for 50 (years).

20. A-dara-[kalama] for 28 (years).

21. A-kur-du-[ana] for 26 (years).

22. Melamma-[kurkura] for 6 (years).

23. Bel-ga[mil?] for 9 (years).

24. For 368 (years) the 11 kings of the dynasty of URU-AZAGGA.

———————

25. Gandis for 16 (years).

26. Agum-si[pak] his son for 22 (years).

27. Guya-si[pak] for 22 (years). 2

28. Ussi his son for 8 (years).

29. Adu-medas for ... (years).

———————

30. Tazzi-gurumas for ... (years).

31. [Agum-kak-rimi ı for ... years].

The next line of this column and the first thirteen lines of the next are destroyed.

COLUMN II

14. ...... for 22 (years).

15. ...... for 26 (years).

16. ...... for 17 (years).

17. Kara ... 2 for 2 (years).

18. Gis-amme ... ti for 6 (years).

19. Saga-sal[tiyas] for 13 (years).

20. Kasbat his son for 8 (years).

2r. Bel-nadin-sumi for 1 year (and) 6 months.

22. Kara-Urus ₃ for 1 year (and) 6 months.

23. Rimmon-nadin-suma for 6 (years).

24. Rimmon-suma-natsir for 30 (years).

25. Meli-Sipak ₄ for 15 (years).

26. Merodach-abla-iddin (Merodach-baladan) his son for 13 (years).

27. Zamama-nadin-sumi ₅ for 1 (year).

28. Bel-suma ... ₆ for 3 (years).

29. For 576 (years) 9 months the 36 kings [of the dynasty of the KASSITES]. ₇

———————

30. Merodach- ... for 17 (years).

31. .... for 6 (years).

The next line of this column and the first four of the next are destroyed.

COLUMN III

5. ...... for 22 (years).

6. Merodach-nadin- ... ₁ for 1 year and 6 months.

7. Merodach-kul[lat] ... ₂ for 13 (years).

8. Nebo-nadin- ... for 9 (years).

9. For 72 (years and) 6 months the 22 kings of the dynasty of ISIN. ₃

———————

10. Simmas-si[pak] for 18 (years).

11. Bel-mukin-[ziri] for 5 months.

12. Kassû-nadin-akhi for 3 (years).

13. For 21 (years and) 5 months the three kings of the dynasty of the land of the Sea. 4

_____

14. E-ulbar-sakin-sumi for 17 (years).

15. Uras-kudurri-[utsur] for 3 (years).

16. Si *lanim* (?)-Sugamu[na] for 3 months.

17. For 20 (years and) 3 months the 3 kings of the dynasty of BIT-[BAZI].

_____

18. AN … [an ELAMITE] for 6 (years).

19. …… for 13 (years).

20. …… for 6 months (and) 12 (days).

The next twelve lines of the column and the first line of the fourth column are destroyed.

COLUMN IV

2. Nebo-suma-yukin [the son of Dakuri] for … (years).

3. Nabu-[natsir] 1 for [14] (years).

4. Nebo-nadin-ziri 2 his son for 2 (years).

5. Nebo-suma-yukin his son for 1 month and 12 days.

6. The 31 [kings?] 3 of the dynasty of BABYLON.

_____

7. Yukin-zira of the dynasty of SASÎ 4 for 3 (years).

8. Pulu ₅ for 2 (years).

9. Ululâ ₆ of the dynasty of TINU for 5 (years).

10. Merodach-abla-iddina (Merodach-baladan) of the dynasty of the country of the Sea for 12 (years).

11. Sargon for 5 (years).

12. Sin-akhe-erba (Sennacherib) of the dynasty of KHABI the greater for 2 (years).

13. Merodach-zakir-sumi the son of Arad-... for 1 month.

14. Merodach-abla-iddina a soldier of KHABI ₇ for 6 months.

15. Bel-ebus of the dynasty of Babylon for 3 (years).

16. Assur-nadin-sumi of the dynasty of KHABI the greater for 6 (years).

17. Nergal-zusezib for 1 (year).

18. Musezib-Merodach of the dynasty of BABYLON for 4 (years).

19. Sin-akhe-erba (Sennacherib) for 8 (years).

20. Assur-akhe-iddina (Esarhaddon) for [12 years].

21. Samas-suma-yukin (Saosdukhinos) for [20 years].

22. Kandal-[anu] (Khineladanos) for [22 years].

The rest of the tablet is destroyed.

Footnotes

15:1 Mr. Pinches' copy gives 36 years.

15:2 Is this king merely a duplicate of his predecessor, the different spelling of the name having caused the annalist to divide one king into two?

16:1 Supplied from an inscription of the king himself, who styles himself the son of Tassi-gurumas, the descendant of Ahi ... the son of Agum. and the offspring of the god Suqamuna.

16:2 Identified by Dr. Oppert with Kudur-Bel, who, according to Nabonidos, was the father of Sagasalti-buryas, the latter of whom reigned 800 years before himself (B.C. 1340). But the identification is doubtful, since the names do not agree.

16:3 "The servant of Bel" (Kudur-Bel) in Kassite.

16:4 "The man of Merodach" in Kassite.

16:5 Zamama-nadin-sumi was a contemporary of the Assyrian king Assur-dan-an (whose name should probably be read Assur-dan, and be identified with that of Assur-dayan, the great-grandfather of Tiglath-Pileser I.)

16:6 Or Bel-nadin- …

16:7 The Kassites were a rude tribe of the Elamite mountains on the northeast side of Babylonia. Nöldeke has shown that they must be identified with the Kossæans of classical geography.

17:1 Perhaps Merodach-nadin-akhi, the antagonist of the Assyrian king Tiglath-Pileser I., 418 years before the conquest of Babylon by Sennacherib, and consequently B.C. 1106.

17:2 Perhaps the Merodach-sapik-kullat of the Synchronous Tablet, who was a contemporary of Assur-bil-kala, the son of Tiglath-Pileser I.

17:3 Isin (PA-SE) was also called Pate'si ("the city of the high-priest" in Babylonia), according to W.A.I., ii. 53, 13.

17:4 That is, the Persian Gulf. Merodach-baladan is described below as also belonging to the dynasty of the country of the Sea, and his ancestral kingdom was that of the Kaldâ or Chaldees in Bit-yagina among the marshes at the mouth of the Euphrates.

18:1 The Nabonassar of Ptolemy's Canon, B.C. 747.

18:2 Called Nadinu in the Babylonian Chronicle.

18:3 Possibly we should supply "years" instead of "kings."

18:4 The annals of Tiglath-Pileser III show that we should read Sapi or Sape. Yukinzira is the Khinziros of Ptolemy's Canon.

18:5 Pulu is the Pul of the Old Testament, the Pôros of Ptolemy's Canon. His name is replaced by that of Tiglath-Pileser in the Babylonian Chronicle, and the two years of his reign correspond with the two years during which Tiglath-Pileser reigned over Babylonia.

18:6 The Shalmaneser of the Babylonian Chronicle and the Assyrian monuments, the Ilulaios of Ptolemy's Canon.

18:7 Does this imply that he was a different person from the famous Merodach-baladan, the contemporary of Sargon and Hezekiah?

No. 3.—TRANSLATION OF THE THIRD DYNASTIC TABLET

Obv.—COLUMN I

Only the ends of two lines in the middle have been preserved.

... 600 (years) he reigned.

[The kings] ... (were) in all.

Obv.—COLUMN II

... ili ......

(AN) Illadu ı the son of the same for ... (years).

Mul-men-nunna ...

Abil (?)-Kis the son of ...

Obv.—COLUMN III

Is entirely lost. It contained about seventy line s.

Rev.—COLUMN IV

[The dynasty] of BABYLON, [11 kings for 294 years].

'Sumu-[abi for 15 years].

Zabû [for 14 years.]

Abil-Sin [for 18 years].

Sin-[muballidh for 30 years].

The next six lines are destroyed.

The 1[1 kings of the dynasty of URU-AZAGGA].

For 3[68 years].

———————

An[man] ...

Ki[-AN-nigas] ...

The rest of the column is destroyed.

Rev.—COLUMN V

The *marshmen* (?) of the country of the sea (were) in all:

———————

The leader of the *marshmen* (?) of the land of the sea (was) Siminas-sipak the son of Erba-Sin;

whose reign was prosperous: his god brought him aid; for 17 years he reigned.

In the palace of Sargon (his corpse) was burned.

Ea-mukin-zira established himself as king, the son of Kha'smar; ₁ for 3 months he reigned.

In the vestments of BIT-KHA'SMAR he was burned.

Kassû-nadin-akhi the son of Sappâ ₂ reigned for 6 years. [He was burned] in the palace.

The 3 kings of the dynasty of the country of the Sea reigned for 23 years.

———————

[E]-ulbar-sakin-sumi the son of Bazi reigned for 15 years: in the palace of KAR-MERODACH [he was burned].

[Uras]-kudurri-utsur the son of Bazi reigned for 2 years.

[Silanim]-Suqamuna the son of Bazi reigned for 3 months: in the palace of LU … SA [he was burned].

———————

[The 3] kings of the dynasty of the house of Bazi reigned for 20 years (and) 3 months.

…… a descendant of the race of ELAM reigned for 6 years.

In the palace of Sargon he was burned.

———————

[One king] of the dynasty of ELAM reigned for 6 years.

The rest of the tablet is lost.

Footnotes

20:1 This was the Semitic reading; the Accadian seems to have been Pallil.

21:1 May also be read Kutmar. The word meant "a hawk" in the Kassite language.

21:2 "The Sappite."

No. 4.—TRANSLATION OF THE BABYLONIAN CHRONICLE

Obv.—COLUMN I

1. [In the 3d year of Nabonassar] king of BABYLON

2. [Tiglath-pileser] in ASSYRIA sat on the throne.

3. In the same year [Tiglath-pileser] descended into the country of ACCAD, and

4. the cities of RABBIKU and KHAMRANU he spoiled,

5. and the gods of the city of SAPAZZA he carried away.

———————

6. In the time of Nabu-natsir (Nabonassar) the town of BORSIPPA

7. was separated from BABYLON. The battle which Nabonassar

8. fought against BORSIPPA is not described. ı

_____

9. In the 5th year of Nabu-natsir Umma(n)-nigas

10. in ELAM sat upon the throne.

_____

11. In (his) 14th year Nabu-natsir fell ill and died ₂ in his palace.

12. For 14 years Nabu-natsir reigned over BABYLON.

13. Nadinu ₃ his son sat upon the throne in BABYLON.

_____

14. In the second year Nadinu was slain in an insurrection.

15. For two years Nadinu reigned over BABYLON.

16. Suma-yukin ₄ the governor, the leader of the insurrection, sat upon the throne.

17. For 2 months and ... days Suma-yukin reigned overBABYLON.

S. Yukin-zira ... seized upon the throne.

_____

19. In the 3d year of Yukin-zira Tiglath-pileser,

20. when he had descended into the country of ACCAD,

21. destroyed BIT-AMUKANU and captured Yukin-zira.

22. For 3 years Yukin-zira reigned over BABYLON.

23. Tiglath-pileser sat upon the throne in BABYLON.

―――――――

24. In (his) 2d year Tiglath-pileser died in the month Tebet. ₁

25. For [22] years Tiglath-pileser the sovereignty over ACCAD

26. and ASSYRIA had exercised. For two years he reigned inACCAD.

27. On the 25th day of the month Tebet Sulman-asarid (Shalmaneser) in ASSYRIA

28. sat upon the throne. He destroyed the city of SABARAHIN. ₂

―――――――

29. In (his) 5th year Sulman-asarid died in the month Tebet.

30. For 5 years Sulman-asarid reigned over the countries ofACCAD and ASSYRIA.

31. On the 12th day of the month Tebet Sargon sat upon the throne in ASSYRIA.

32. In the month Nisan Merodach-baladan sat upon the throne inBABYLON.

―――――――

33. In the 2d year of Merodach-baladan Umma(n)-nigas king of Elam

34. in the province of DUR-ILI fought a battle against Sargon king of ASSYRIA, and

35. caused a revolt from ASSYRIA: he overthrew them ₁ utterly.

36. Merodach-baladan and his army, which to the assistance

37. of the king of ELAM had gone, did not obtain a battle: he arrived too late. ₂

―――――――

38. In the 5th year of Merodach-baladan Umma(n)-nigas king ofELAM died.

39. [For 3 years] Umma(n)-nigas reigned over ELAM.

40. [Sutruk ₃-nankhun]du the son of his sister sat on the throne in ELAM.

41. ...... up to the 10th year

The remaining lines of the column are destroyed.

COLUMN II

1. In the ... th year ...

2. A battle ...

3. For 12 years [Merodach-baladan reigned over BABYLON]. 4

4. Sargon [sat upon. the throne in BABYLON].4

The next fourteen lines are destroyed.

19. The Babylonians he did not *oppress* (?) 5 ...

20. he (Sennacherib) was angry also with Merodach-baladan, and [took him prisoner];

2 I. he devastated his country, and ...

22. the cities of LARAK and SARRABA[NU 6 he destroyed].

23. After his capture (Sennacherib) placed Bel-ibni upon the throne in BABYLON.

---

24. In the first year of Bel-ibni Sennacherib.

25. destroyed the cities of KHIRIMMA and KHARARATUM.

---

26. In the 3d year of Bel-ibni Sennacherib into the country ofACCAD

27. descended, and devastated the country of ACCAD.

28. Bel-ibni and his officers he transported into ASSYRIA.

29. For 3 years Bel-ibni reigned over BABYLON.

30. Sennacherib his son, Assur-nadin-suma

31. placed upon the throne in BABYLON.

32. In the first year of Assur-nadin-suma Sutruk-[nan]khundu ₁king of ELAM

33. was seized by his brother Khallusu who closed the gate before him. ₂

34. For 18 years Sutruk-[nan]khundu had reigned over ELAM.

35. His brother Khallusu sat upon the throne in ELAM.

---

36. In the 6th year of Assur-nadin-suma Sennacherib

37. descended into the country of ELAM, and the cities ofNAGITUM, KHILMI,

38. PELLATUM and KHUPAPANU he destroyed.

39. He carried away their spoil. Afterwards Khallusu the king ofELAM

40. marched into the country of ACCAD and entered Sippara on the *march* (?).

41. He killed some people (but) the Sun-god did not issue forth from the temple of E-BABARA.

42. He captured Assur-nadin-suma and he was carried to ELAM.

43. For 6 years Assur-nadin-suma reigned over BABYLON.

44. The king of ELAM placed Nergal-yusezib in BABYLON

45. on the throne. He caused [a revolt] from ASSYRIA.

---

46. In the 1st year of Nergal-yusezib, on the 16th day of the month Tammuz, ₁

47. Nergal-yusezib captured NIPUR ₂ and occupied its *neighbourhood* (?).

48. On the first day of the month Tammuz the soldiers ofASSYRIA had entered URUK. ₃

COLUMN III

1. They spoiled the gods belonging to URUK as well as its inhabitants.

2. Nergal-yusezib fled after the Elamites, and the gods belonging to URUK

3. as well as its inhabitants (the Assyrians) carried away. On the 7th day of the month Tisri 4 in the province of NIPUR

4. he fought a battle against the soldiers of ASSYRIA and was taken prisoner in the conflict, and

5. he was carried to ASSYRIA. For 1 year and 6 months Nergal-yusezib

6. reigned over BABYLON. On the 26th day of the [month Tisri?]

7. against Khallusu king of ELAM his people revolted, [the gate before] him

8. they closed. They slew him. For 6 years Khallusu reigned over ELAM.

9. Kudur in ELAM sat upon the throne. Afterwards Sennacherib

10. descended into ELAM and from the country of RASI as far as

11. BIT-BURNA 5 he devastated.

12. Musezib-Merodach sat upon the throne in BABYLON.

13. In the first year of Musezib-Merodach on the 17th day of the month Ab 1

14. Kudur king of ELAM was seized in an insurrection and killed. For 10 months

15. Kudur had reigned over ELAM. Menanu in ELAM

16. sat upon the throne. I do not know the year 2 when the soldiers of ELAM and ACCAD

17. he collected together and in the city of KHALULE a battle against ASSYRIA

18. he fought, and caused a revolt from Assyria. 3

19. In the 4th year of Musezib-Merodach on the 15th day of Nisan 4

20. Menanu king of ELAM was paralysed, 5 and

21. his mouth was seized and he was deprived of speech.

22. On the first day of the month Kisleu 6 the city [of BABYLON] was taken, Musezib-Merodach

23. was taken and led away to ASSYRIA.

24. For 4 years Musezib-Merodach reigned over BABYLON.

25. On the 7th day of the month Adar 7 Menanu king of ELAMdied.

26. For 4 years Menanu reigned over ELAM.

27. Khumma-khaldasu 8 in ELAM sat upon the throne.

---

28. In the eighth year of the king there was … in Babylon. On the 3d day of the month Tammuz

29. the gods belonging to ERECH went down from the city OfERIDU 9 to ERECH.

30. On the 3d day of the month Tisri Khumma-khaldasu the king of ELAM by the Fire-god

31. was stricken and perished through the *power* (?) of the god. For 8 years Khumma-khaldasu

32. reigned over ELAM.

33. Khumma-khaldasu the second in the country of ELAM sat upon the throne.

34. On the 10th day of the month Tebet, 1 Sennacherib king ofASSYRIA

35. by his own son 2 was murdered in an insurrection. For [24] years Sennacherib

36. reigned over Assyria. From the 20th day of the month Tebet until

37. the 2d day of the month Adar is described as a period of insurrection in ASSYRIA.

38. On the 8th day of the month Sivan 3 Assur-akhi-iddina (Esar-haddon) his son sat on the throne in ASSYRIA.

39. In the first year of Esar-haddon, Zira-kina-esir ₄ of the sea coast, ₅

40. when he had laid fetters on the city of ERECH, the city. of [ERECH?]

41. destroyed in sight of the officers of ASSYRIA and [fled] to the country of ELAM.

42. In ELAM the king of ELAM took him and [slew him] with the sword.

43. In a month I do not know the officer called *Gu-enna* was ... in the city of NIPUR.

---

44. In the month Elul, ₆ the god Gu'si ₇ and the gods [of the city of ...]

45. proceeded to DUR-ILI; [the gods of ......]

46. proceeded to DUR-SARGON ......

47. In the month Adar the heads of ......

---

48. In the second year the major-domo ......

The next two lines are destroyed.

Rev.—COLUMN IV

1. ...... akhe-sullim the *Gu-enna.*

2... [the Gimir]ri ₁ marched against ASSYRIA and in ASSYRIA were slain.

3... the city of SIDON was taken; its spoil was carried away.

4. The major-domo mustered a gathering in ACCAD.

---

5. In the 5th year on the 2d day of the month Tisri the Assyrian soldiers BAZZA ₂

6. occupied. In the month Tisri the head of the king of the country of SIDON

7. was cut off, and brought to Assyria. In the month Adar the head of the king

8. of the countries of GUNDU and 'SI'SÛ 3 was cut off and brought to ASSYRIA.

---

9. In the 6th year the king of ELAM entered SIPPARA. He offered sacrifices. The Sun-god 4 from

10. the temple of E-BABARA did not issue forth. The Assyrians marched into EGYPT. ETHIOPIA was troubled. 5

11. Khumma-khaldasu the king of ELAM without being sick died in his palace.

12. For 5 years Khumma-khaldasu reigned over ELAM.

13. Urtagu his brother sat upon the throne in ELAM.

14. In a month I do not know Nadin-Suma the *Gu-enna*

15. and Kudur the son of Dakuri went to ASSYRIA.

---

16. In the 7th year on the 5th day of the month Adar the soldiers of ASSYRIA marched into EGYPT.

17. In the month Adar Istar of the city of ACCAD and the gods of the city of ACCAD

18. had departed from the country of ELAM and on the 10th day of the month Adar entered the city of ACCAD.

---

19. In the 8th year of Esar-haddon in the month Tebet on a day of which the date has been lost 1

20. the country of the RURIZÂ was occupied; its spoil was carried away.

21. In the month Kisleu its spoil was brought into the city of UR.

22. On the 5th day of the month Adar the wife of the king died.

23. In the tenth year in the month Nisan the soldiers of ASSYRIAmarched into Egypt. 2

24. On the 3d day of the month Tammuz and also on the 16th and 18th days

25. three times the Egyptians were defeated with heavy loss. 3

26. On the 22d day Memphis, 4 the royal city, was captured.

27. Its king fled; his son descended into the country of [ETHIOPIA].

28. Its spoil was carried away; [its] men were [enslaved]; its goods were ......

---

29. In the 11th year the king [remained] in ASSYRIA; his officers ......

---

30. In the 12th year the king of ASSYRIA ......

31. On the march he fell ill, and died on the 10th day of the month Marchesvan. 1

32. For 12 years Esar-haddon reigned over ASSYRIA.

33. Saul-suma-yukina in BABYLON, Assur-bani-pal in ASSYRIA, his two sons, sat on the throne.

---

34. In the accession year of Saul-suma-yukina in the month Iyyar, 2

35. Bel and the gods of ACCAD from the city of ASSUR

36. had gone forth and on the 11th day of the month Iyyar had entered into BABYLON.

37. In that year [against] the city of KIRBITUM 3 [there was war]; its king is conquered.

38. On the 10th day of the month Tebet Bel-edir- *nisi* (?) inBABYLON is seized and put to death.

---

39. The first part (of the chronicle) has been written like its original and has been made public.

40. The tablet of Ana-Bel-KAN the son of Libludhu

41. the son of Nis-Sin, by the hand of Ea-iddin the son of

42. Ana-Bel-KAN the son of Libludhu of Babylon,

43. the 5th day of the month ... the 22d year of Darius king ofBABYLON,

44. the king of the world.

Footnotes

22:1 That is, in the history from which the writer extracted his chronicles.

22:2 Literally "fate" (overtook him).

22:3 The Nebo-nadin-ziri ("Nebo has given a seed") of the Dynastic Tablet; Nadios in Ptolemy's Canon.

22:4 Called Nebo-suma-yukin in the Dynastic Tablet.

23:1 December.

23:2 Not to be confounded with 'Samerina or Samaria. M. Halévy may be right in identifying it with the city of Sibraim mentioned in Ezek. xlvii. 16 as lying between Damascus and Hamath.

24:1 That is, the Assyrians. The Annals of Sargon, on the other hand, claim the victory for Assyria, though Babylonia was left in the hands of Merodach-baladan.

24:2 Literally, "he undertook it too late" (*ana arki itsbat-'sa*).

24:3 The Elamite Sutruk was identified by the Assyrians with their goddess Istar.

24:4 So restored by Winckler.

24:5 *Ikhmi's*.

24:6 See W.A.I., ii. 69, No. 5, 13. Larak was the Larankha of Berossos, which the Greek writer seems to have confounded with Surippak near Sippara.

25:1 Written Is-tar-khu-un-du. The Susian inscriptions of the king himself write the name Su-ut-ru-uk-[AN]-Nakh-khu-un-te.

25:2 That is, imprisoned him.

26:1 June.

26:2 Now Niffer.

26:3 Now Warka, the Erech of Gen. x. 10.

26:4 September.

26:5 Bit-Burna (-KI) is called Bit Buna (-KI) in the annals of Sennacherib.

27:1 July.

27:2 The chronicler's sources here failed him, but Winckler has pointed out that the battle of Khalule must have taken place in either B.C. 691 or 690.

27:3 The annals of Sennacherib claim a complete victory for the Assyrians.

27:4 March.

27:5 Literally, "Tetanus constricted him" (*misidtuv imisid*, cf. W.A.I., ii. 27. 47, 48).

27:6 November.

27:7 February.

27:8 Called Umman-aldas in the Assyrian inscriptions.

27:9 Eridu was on the coast of the Persian Gulf.

28:1 December.

28:2 It will be noticed that the chronicler speaks of only one son, whereas two are named in the Old Testament.

28:3 May.

28:4 Called by Esar-haddon Nebo-zira-kina-esir ("Nebo has directed the established seed"), the son of Merodach-baladan.

28:5 That is, of the Persian Gulf.

28:6 August.

28:7 "The god of the favourable mouth," a local divinity (perhaps belonging to Sippara, W.A.I., v. 3r, 30), and identified with Uras (W.A.I., ii. 57, 54).

29:1 So restored by Winckler. The Gimirrâ are the Gomer of the Old Testament, the Kimmerians of classical writers.

29:2 Apparently the district of Arabia Petræa called Bazu by Esar-haddon, Buz in the Old Testament.

29:3 Probably in Kilikia.

29:4 The Sun-god whose temple has been discovered by Mr. Hormuzd Rassam in the mounds of Abu-Habba was the patron-deity of Sipar or Sippara. Besides "Sippara of the Sun-god," there was a neighbouring city called "Sippara of Anunit." The two together formed the Scriptural Sepharvaim or "two Sipparas."

29:5 *Melukh imina.*

30:1 In the history from which the chronicler derived his account.

30:2 The chronicler notes here that the last character in the line was wanting in his copy.

30:3 Literally, "massacres took place in Egypt."

30:4 Written *Membi.*

31:1 October.

31:2 April.

31:3 Apparently the city of Karbat in Northern Egypt, conquered by Assur-bani-pal at the commencement of his reign.

No. 5.—TRANSLATION OF THE INSCRIPTION GIVING THE ASSYRIAN INTERPRETATION OF THE NAMES OF THE EARLY BABYLONIAN KINGS

Obv.—COLUMN I

About forty lines lost.

1. [? Ur-Damu. *Acc.* 1]	"Man of the goddess GULA."
2. [? Babar-uru. *Acc.*]	"The Sun-god protects."
3. [Ur- ...]la. *Acc.*	"Man of the Moon-god."
4. [Ur-]Babara. *Acc.*	"Man of the Sun-god."
5. [Is-ki-]pal. *Acc.*	"Sweeper away of the hostile country."
6. [Gul-ki-]sar. *Acc.*	"Destroyer of hosts."
7. A-[dara]-kalama. *Acc.*	"Son of the god EA king of the land."
8. A-kur-du-ana. *Acc.*	"Son of BEL (the mountain) of the treasury of heaven."
9. Lugal-ginna. *Acc.*	"Established king"(Sargon). 2
10. The queen Azag-Bau. *Acc.*	"The goddess BAU is holy."

---

11. These are the kings who after the flood are not described in chronological order.

---

12. Khammu-ragas. *Kas.* 3	"Of a large family."
13. Ammi-didugga. *Kas.*	"Of an established family."
14. Kur-gal-zu. *Kas.*	"Be a shepherd."
15. Simmas-sipak. *Kas.*	"Offspring of MERODACH."
16. Ulam-bur-yas. *Kas.*	"Offspring of the lord of the world."
17. Nazi-Murudas. *Kas.*	"The shadow of URAS."
18. Meli-Sipak. *Kas.*	"Man of MERODACH."
19. Burna-bur-yas. *Kas.*	"Servant [of the lord of the world]."
20. Kara-Urus. *Kas.*	"Minister of [BEL]."

COLUMN II

About thirty-three lines are lost.

1. [an-]khegal. *Acc.*	"With MERODACH is life."
2. [an-]khegal. *Acc.*	"With MERODACH is verdure."
3. Lu-Silig-lu-sar. *Acc.*	"Man of MERODACH."
4. Un-kur-Silig-alim. *Acc.*	"The lord of the land is MERODACH."
5. Gu-sermal-Tutu. *Acc.*	"The closer of the mouth is MERODACH."
6. Sazu-[AN]kusvu. *Acc.*	"MERODACH is an over-shadowing god."
7. Sazu-ap-tila-nen-gu. *Acc.*	"MERODACH has declared life to him."
8. Ur-Nin-din-bagga. *Acc.*	"Man of GULA [the goddess of life and death]."
9. Khumeme. *Acc.*	"Man of GULA."

10. Dili-khidu. *Acc.*	"(Man of) the god PAPSUKAL." 1
11. Mu-na-tila. *Acc.*	"May his name live."
12. Nannak-satu. *Acc.*	"The Moon-god has begotten."
13. Nannak-agal-duabi. *Acc.*	"The Moon-god is strong over all."
14. Labar-Nu-dimmud. *Acc.*	"Servant of EA [lord of the universe]."
15. Urudu-man-sun. *Acc.*	"The god NUSKU has given."
16. Kud-ur-Alima. *Acc.*	"Sweet are the loins of BEL."
17. Dun-aga-ba-khe-til. *Acc.*	"May BAU vivify her womb."
18. Damu-mu-as-khe-gal. *Acc.*	"May GULA be one name."
19. Dun-gal-tur-taê. *Acc.*	"May BAU establish great and small."
20. Tutu-bul-anta-gal. *Acc.*	"O MERODACH as a comrade spare her (?)."
21. Dugga-makh-Sazu. *Acc.*	"Supreme is the word of MERODACH."
22. Khedu-lamma-ra. *Acc.*	"PAP-SUKAL is the colossus."
23. Mul-khe-sal. *Acc.*	"May BEL be exalted."
24. Dimir-Uru-du. *Acc.*	"The Moon-god as son [of the city UR]."
25. Dimir-Uruk-du. *Acc.*	"The god who is the son of [ERECH]."
26. Dimir-Erida-du-ru. *Acc.*	"EA [as son of ERIDU, the creator]."

The next two lines are destroyed.

Rev.—COLUMN III

The first two lines are destroyed.

1. … a-edina. *Acc.*	"The choir of the goddess ZARPANIT."
2. 'Si-ru. *Acc.*	"BEL has created."
3. Kur-nigin-garra-gurus-nene. *Acc.*	"URAS is their first-born."
4. Uras-saglitar ı-zae-men. *Acc.*	"URAS, thou art overseer."
5. Uras-qalzi-nes-kiam-mama. *Acc.*	"URAS who loves constancy."
6. Mul-lil-ki-bi-gi. *Acc.*	"BEL of Nipur has returned to his place."
7. Laghlaghghi-Gar. *Acc.*	"NEBO illuminates."
8. Kur-gal-nin-mu-pada. *Acc.*	"The great mountain (BEL) records the name."
9. Aba-Sanabi-dari. *Acc.*	"Who is like BEL a bridegroom."
10. Aba-Sanabi-diri. *Acc.*	"Who is like BEL (the lord) of counsel."
11. Es-Guzi-gin-du. *Acc.*	"The temple of E-SAGGIL the establishment of the son."
12. Khu-un-zuh. *Acc.*	"BEL who knows mankind."
13. Nab-sakh-menna. *Acc.*	"BEL, prosper me."
14. Massu-gal-Babara-gude. *Acc.*	"What is shorn by RIMMON."
15. Ur-Sanabi. *Acc.*	"The man of EA."
16. Lu-Damu. *Acc.*	"The man of GULA."
17. Tutul-Savul. *Acc.*	"The Sun-god has mustered."

18. Nin-sakh-gu-nu-tatal. *Acc.*	"PAP-SUKAL who changes not (his) command."
19. Agu-sag-algi. *Acc.*	"The Moon-god has given a son." ₁
20. Agu-ba-tila. *Acc.*	"May the Moon-god vivify what is below him."
21. Larru-ningub-al. *Acc.*	"O BEL, defend the landmark."
22. Lubar-E-gir-azagga. *Acc.*	"Servant of NERGAL."
23. Bad-Mullilla. *Acc.*	"Minister of BEL."
24. Nanak-gula. *Acc.*	"The Moon-god is great."
25. … nu-laragh-danga-su-mu-aldibba. *Acc.*	"(O Sun-)god, in difficulties and dangers take my hand."
26. [ES-Guzi-]kharsag-men. *Acc.*	"E-SAGGIL is our mountain."

More than thirty lines are destroyed here.

COLUMN IV

1. Ulam-Urus. *Kas.*	"Offspring of BEL."
2. Meli-Khali. *Kas.*	"Man of GULA."
3. Meli-Sumu. *Kas.*	"Man of the god SUQAMUNA."
4. Meli-Sibarru. *Kas.*	"Man of the god SIMALIA."
5. Meli-Sakh. *Kas.*	"Man of the Sun-god."
6. Nimgirabi. *Kas.*	"The merciful."
7. Nimgirabi-Sakh. *Kas.*	"Merciful is the Sun-god."
8. Nimgirabi-Buryas. *Kas.*	"Merciful is [BEL the lord of the world]."
9. Kara-Buryas. *Kas.*	"Servant of [BEL lord of the world]."
10. Kara-Sakh. *Kas.*	"Servant of the Sun-god."
11. Nazi-Sipak. *Kas.*	["Shadow of MERODACH."]
12. Nazi-Buryas. *Kas.*	["Shadow of BEL lord] of the world."

The remaining eight lines are lost.

Footnotes

32:1 That is, Accado-Sumerian.

32:2 The name of the king was really Sarganu (perhaps of the same origin as the Biblical Serug), but his Accadian subjects misunderstood it, turning it into Sarru-kinu, "established king," which was written in Sumerian Lugal-ginna.

32:3 That is, Kassite or Kossæan.

33:1 Literally "the messenger of the treasury (of heaven)."

34:1 The correct reading of this word is doubtful.

35:1 The Assyro-Babylonian translation is a paraphrase, as in some other instances. The Accado-Sumerian compound is literally: "The Moon-god has established a head."

No. 6.—TRANSLATION OF THE ANNALS OF SARGON OF ACCAD AND NARAM-SIN 1

OBVERSE

1. When the moon at its setting with the colour of a dust-cloud 2 filled the crescent, the moon was favourable for Sargon who at this season

2. marched against the country of ELAM and subjugated the men of ELAM.

3. Misery (?) he brought upon them; their food he cut off.

---

4. When the moon at its setting filled the crescent with the colour of a dust-cloud, and over the face of the sky the colour extended behind the moon during the day and remained bright,

5. the moon was favourable for Sargon who marched against the country of [PHŒNICIA], and

6. subjugated the country of PHŒNICIA. His hand conquered the four quarters (of the world).

---

7. When the moon increased in form on the right hand and on the left, and moreover [during] the day the finger reached over the horns, 3

8. the moon was favourable for Sargon who at this season produced *joy* (?) [in] BABYLON, and

9. [like] dust the spoil of BAB-DHUNA was carried away and

10. ... he made ACCAD a city; the city of ... he called its name;

11. [the men of ... in the] midst he caused to dwell.

---

12. [When the moon] on the left the colour of fire [on] the left of the planet, and

13. [the moon was favourable to Sargo]n who at this season against the country of PHŒNICIA

14. [marched and subjugated it]. The four quarters (of the world) his hand conquered.

---

15. [When the moon] behind the moon the four heads were placed,

16. [the moon was favourable to Sargon who at this season] marched [against] the country of PHŒNICIA and

17. [subjugated the country of PHŒNICIA.] His [enemies?] he smote; his heroes

18. ....in the gate of its ₁ rising.

---

19. [When the moon was fixed?] and a span [the moon was favourable to Sargon] as for whom at this season the goddess [ISHTAR]

20. [with favours] filled for him his hand the goddess ISHTAR [all countries]

21. caused him to conquer; against Tiri (?) ...

---

22. [When the moon] appeared [like] a lion, the moon was favourable to Sargon who at this season

23. was [very] exalted and a rival (or) equal had not; his own country was at peace. Over

24. [the countries] of the sea of the setting sun ₂ he crossed and for 3 years at the setting sun

25. [all countries] his hand conquered. Every place to form but one (empire) he appointed. His images at the setting sun

26. he erected. Their spoil he caused to pass over into the countries of the sea. ₁

27. [When the moon on] the right hand was like the colour of gall, and there was no finger; ₂ the upper part was long and the moon was setting (?),

28. [the moon was favourable for] Sargon who enlarged his palace of Delight (?) by 5 *mitkhu*, and

29. established the chiefs [in it] and called it the House of *Kiâm-izallik*. ₃

---

30. When the moon was like a *cloud* (?), like the colour of gall, and there was no finger; ₂ on the right side was the colour of a sword; the circumference of the left side was visible;

31. towards its face on the left the colour extended; the moon was favourable for Sargon against whom at this season Kastubila of the country of KAZALLA rebelled and against KAZALLA

32. (Sargon) marched and he smote their forces; he accomplished their destruction.

33. Their mighty army he annihilated; he reduced KAZALLA to dust and ruins.

34. The station of the birds ₄ he overthrew.

---

35. When the moon was like a *cloud* (?), like the colour of gall, and there was no finger; ₁ on the right side was the colour of a sword; the circumference of the left was visible;

36. and against its face the Seven ₂ advanced; the moon was favourable to Sargon, against whom at this season

37. the elders of the whole country revolted and besieged him in the city of ACCAD; but

38. Sargon issued forth and smote their forces; their destruction he accomplished.

REVERSE

1. Their numerous soldiery he massacred; the spoil that was upon them he collected.

2. "The booty of Istar!" he shouted.

---

3. When the moon had two fingers, and swords were seen on the right side and the left, [and] might and peace were on the left

4. its hand presented a sword; the sword in its left hand was of the colour of *'sukhuruni;* the point was held in the left hand and there were two heads;

5. [the moon] was favourable for Sargon who at this season

6. subjected the men of [the country] of 'SU-EDIN 3 in its plenitude to the sword, and

7. Sargon caused their seats to be occupied, and

8. smote their forces; their destruction he accomplished; their mighty army

9. he cut off, and his troops he collected; into the city of ACCAD he brought (them) back.

---

10. [When the moon] had two fingers and on the right side it was of the colour of a sword and on the left it was visible;

11. [and against its face] the Seven advanced; (its) appearance was of the colour of gall; the moon was favourable for Naram-Sin

12. [who at] this season marched against the city of APIRAK, and

13. [utterly] destroyed it: Ris-Rimmon the king of APIRAK

14. [he overthrew], and the city of APIRAK his hand conquered.

---

15. [When the moon] on the right it was of the colour of a sword, and on the left it was visible;

16. [and against its face the Seven advanced?]; the moon was favourable for Naram-Sin who at this season

17. marched [against the country of MÂ]GANNA ı and seized the country of MÂGANNA, and

18 the king of MÂGANNA his hand captured.

---

19. [When against the moon] the Seven were banded, [and] behind it

20. ...... never may there be a son (?) ......

Footnotes

37:1 W.A.I., iv. 34. The text has been translated in part by Mr. George Smith. The astrological notices with which the account of Sargon's campaigns is associated are explained by the fact that the great Chaldean work on astronomy and astrology was compiled for his library at Accad, and that one of the objects of this work was to trace a connection between certain astronomical occurrences and the events which immediately followed them.

37:2 *Ana pikhirti-su tsirip zakiki.*

37:3 The moon lay on its back, and the distance from the extremity of one horn to that of another was as much as a span.

38:1 The Sun-god must be referred to.

38:2 The Mediterranean.

39:1 We infer from this that Sargon had crossed over into Cyprus, and there erected an image of himself. This might explain why his later namesake Sargon sent to the island a monument, which is now in Berlin. General di Cesnola brought back from Cyprus a Babylonian cylinder of hæmatite bearing the inscription, "Abil-Istar, the son of Ilu-Balidh, the servant of the deified Naram-Sin." The cylinder was probably executed either during the reign of Naram-Sin, or shortly afterwards, as the cult of the king is not likely to have continued after the fall of his dynasty.

39:2 It could not be measured.

39:3 "Thus he has appointed."

39:4 What this refers to it is impossible to say. The expression can hardly be metaphorical.

40:1 It could not be measured.

40:2 The Seven Evil Spirits who were supposed to cause eclipses of the moon.

40:3 "The plain of the 'Suti," or nomad tribes on the eastern side of Babylonia.

41:1 The Sinaitic Peninsula.

No. 6.—TRANSLATION OF THE ANNALS OF SARGON OF ACCAD AND NARAM-SIN 1

OBVERSE

1. When the moon at its setting with the colour of a dust-cloud 2filled the crescent, the moon was favourable for Sargon who at this season

2. marched against the country of ELAM and subjugated the men of ELAM.

3. Misery (?) he brought upon them; their food he cut off.

――――――

4. When the moon at its setting filled the crescent with the colour of a dust-cloud, and over the face of the sky the colour extended behind the moon during the day and remained bright,

5. the moon was favourable for Sargon who marched against the country of [PHŒNICIA], and

6. subjugated the country of PHŒNICIA. His hand conquered the four quarters (of the world).

――――――

7. When the moon increased in form on the right hand and on the left, and moreover [during] the day the finger reached over the horns, 3

8. the moon was favourable for Sargon who at this season produced *joy* (?) [in] BABYLON, and

9. [like] dust the spoil of BAB-DHUNA was carried away and

10. ... he made ACCAD a city; the city of ... he called its name;

11. [the men of ... in the] midst he caused to dwell.

_____

12. [When the moon] on the left the colour of fire [on] the left of the planet, and

13. [the moon was favourable to Sargo]n who at this season against the country of PHŒNICIA

14. [marched and subjugated it]. The four quarters (of the world) his hand conquered.

_____

15. [When the moon] behind the moon the four heads were placed,

16. [the moon was favourable to Sargon who at this season] marched [against] the country of PHŒNICIA and

17. [subjugated the country of PHŒNICIA.] His [enemies?] he smote; his heroes

18. ....in the gate of its ı rising.

_____

19. [When the moon was fixed?] and a span [the moon was favourable to Sargon] as for whom at this season the goddess [ISHTAR]

20. [with favours] filled for him his hand the goddess ISHTAR [all countries]

21. caused him to conquer; against Tiri (?) ...

_____

22. [When the moon] appeared [like] a lion, the moon was favourable to Sargon who at this season

23. was [very] exalted and a rival (or) equal had not; his own country was at peace. Over

24. [the countries] of the sea of the setting sun ₂ he crossed and for 3 years at the setting sun

25. [all countries] his hand conquered. Every place to form but one (empire) he appointed. His images at the setting sun

26. he erected. Their spoil he caused to pass over into the countries of the sea. ₁

---

27. [When the moon on] the right hand was like the colour of gall, and there was no finger; ₂ the upper part was long and the moon was setting (?),

28. [the moon was favourable for] Sargon who enlarged his palace of Delight (?) by 5 *mitkhu*, and

29. established the chiefs [in it] and called it the House of *Kiâm-izallik*. ₃

---

30. When the moon was like a *cloud* (?), like the colour of gall, and there was no finger; ₂ on the right side was the colour of a sword; the circumference of the left side was visible;

31. towards its face on the left the colour extended; the moon was favourable for Sargon against whom at this season Kastubila of the country of KAZALLA rebelled and againstKAZALLA

32. (Sargon) marched and he smote their forces; he accomplished their destruction.

33. Their mighty army he annihilated; he reduced KAZALLA to dust and ruins.

34. The station of the birds ₄ he overthrew.

---

35. When the moon was like a *cloud* (?), like the colour of gall, and there was no finger; ₁ on the right side was the colour of a sword; the circumference of the left was visible;

36. and against its face the Seven ₂ advanced; the moon was favourable to Sargon, against whom at this season

37. the elders of the whole country revolted and besieged him in the city of ACCAD; but

38. Sargon issued forth and smote their forces; their destruction he accomplished.

REVERSE

1. Their numerous soldiery he massacred; the spoil that was upon them he collected.

2. "The booty of Istar!" he shouted.

---

3. When the moon had two fingers, and swords were seen on the right side and the left, [and] might and peace were on the left

4. its hand presented a sword; the sword in its left hand was of the colour of 'sukhuruni; the point was held in the left hand and there were two heads;

5. [the moon] was favourable for Sargon who at this season

6. subjected the men of [the country] of 'SU-EDIN ₃ in its plenitude to the sword, and

7. Sargon caused their seats to be occupied, and

8. smote their forces; their destruction he accomplished; their mighty army

9. he cut off, and his troops he collected; into the city of ACCADhe brought (them) back.

---

10. [When the moon] had two fingers and on the right side it was of the colour of a sword and on the left it was visible;

11. [and against its face] the Seven advanced; (its) appearance was of the colour of gall; the moon was favourable for Naram-Sin

12. [who at] this season marched against the city of APIRAK, and

13. [utterly] destroyed it: Ris-Rimmon the king of APIRAK

14. [he overthrew], and the city of APIRAK his hand conquered.

15. [When the moon] on the right it was of the colour of a sword, and on the left it was visible;

16. [and against its face the Seven advanced?]; the moon was favourable for Naram-Sin who at this season

17. marched [against the country of MÂ]GANNA ₁ and seized the country of MÂGANNA, and

18 the king of MÂGANNA his hand captured.

---

19. [When against the moon] the Seven were banded, [and] behind it

20. ...... never may there be a son (?) ......

Footnotes

37:1 W.A.I., iv. 34. The text has been translated in part by Mr. George Smith. The astrological notices with which the account of Sargon's campaigns is associated are explained by the fact that the great Chaldean work on astronomy and astrology was compiled for his library at Accad, and that one of the objects of this work was to trace a connection between certain astronomical occurrences and the events which immediately followed them.

37:2 *Ana pikhirti-su tsirip zakiki.*

37:3 The moon lay on its back, and the distance from the extremity of one horn to that of another was as much as a span.

38:1 The Sun-god must be referred to.

38:2 The Mediterranean.

39:1 We infer from this that Sargon had crossed over into Cyprus, and there erected an image of himself. This might explain why his later namesake Sargon sent to the island a monument, which is now in Berlin. General di Cesnola brought back from Cyprus a Babylonian cylinder of hæmatite bearing the inscription, "Abil-Istar, the son of Ilu-Balidh, the servant of the deified Naram-Sin." The cylinder was probably executed either during the reign of Naram-Sin, or shortly afterwards, as the cult of the king is not likely to have continued after the fall of his dynasty.

39:2 It could not be measured.

39:3 "Thus he has appointed."

39:4 What this refers to it is impossible to say. The expression can hardly be metaphorical.

40:1 It could not be measured.

40:2 The Seven Evil Spirits who were supposed to cause eclipses of the moon.

40:3 "The plain of the 'Suti," or nomad tribes on the eastern side of Babylonia.

41:1 The Sinaitic Peninsula.

THE INSCRIPTIONS OF TELLOH—INTRODUCTION

By M. Arthur Amiaud

THE names of Telloh and of the French Consul M. de Sarzec are no longer strange to the Orientalist of to-day. The situation of the mounds, which have hidden and preserved to our day the ruins of one of the most ancient centres of civilisation, is well known. The history of the excavations has been often written, and I shall not dwell upon it. Nor shall I discuss the results of these excavations front the point of view of art or archæology. This work has been undertaken by a master hand in the *Découvertes en Chaldée.* 1 At present I shall only essay to follow in the steps of Dr. Oppert by making the monuments of stone and brick tell their own tale, and by questioning them summarily on the geography, history, politics, and religion of their age and country. 2

I. The first question one thinks of asking is what was the name of that flourishing city of ancient Chaldæa which the Bedouin now knows only as Telloh? Considering that all the princes whose names occur on the monuments are entitled "kings" or "patesis" of *Shirpurla-ki*, it was generally answered at first: This city was Shirpurla. 1 As often happens, the first impression has proved to be correct. I was wrong in questioning the identification in an article in the *Zeitschrift für Keilschriftforschung* (i. p. 151). I had remarked that except in the title of the kings and patesis the name of Shirpurla-ki appeared very rarely in the inscriptions of Telloh, and that whenever a prince mentioned the site where a temple was erected he gave it another name—Girsu-ki,

Uru-azagga, Ninâ-ki, Gishgalla-ki. I now believe, and shall attempt to prove, that Telloh really represents the ruins of Shirpurla; that it was the general name of a great centre of population, of which Girsu-ki, Uru-azagga, Ninâ-ki, and Gishgalla-ki were only divisions or quarters.

Let us first remove a hypothesis which could present itself to the mind. Might not Shirpurla be the name of a country, of which Girsu-ki and the three other cities mentioned above were the chief places? This supposition is forbidden by the inscription of the statue F of Gudea, which states formally that Shirpurla was the beloved "city" of the goddess Gatumdug (col. i., cases 15, 16). It is also forbidden by W.A.I., ii. 61, 2, 37, where we learn that a temple otherwise unknown was situated in Shirpurla-ki.

The list of temples given in this passage might open the door to another hypothesis, which must be removed in its turn, for it would be inconsistent with the relations existing between Shirpurla and the four other towns. In lines 34 and 35 two temples are named as temples of Girsu-ki. If Girsu-ki had been only a quarter of Shirpurla, would there not be some inconsistency on the part of the Assyrian scribe in saying: Such and such temples belong to Girsu-ki, such another to Shirpurla-ki? Might one not conclude that Shirpurla and the four other towns were separate cities?

Now it is certain that Gudea tells us (in the inscription on statue C) that he has constructed the temple of E-anna for the goddess Ninni or Istar in Girsu-ki (col. 3, cases 11, 12). We further know that the same Istar, the presiding deity of Erech, had a celebrated temple in that city which also bore the name of E-anna. Moreover, certain texts of Gudea and Dungi, which mention the construction of temples in Girsu-ki, come, it is believed, from other sites than Telloh, some from Warka or Erech, others from Babylon, from Zerghul and from Tel-Eed. But this proves nothing in favour of Erech, and still less against Telloh. From the fact that Istar had a temple named E-anna at Erech, we cannot infer that the same goddess had not a temple of the same name in another city. We know that Nebo had a temple called E-Zida in Borsippa, and there were at least two others of the same name at Babylon and Calah.

We cannot look for Ninâ-ki, any more than Girsu-ki, outside Telloh, or identify it with the Assyrian Nineveh. [1] As for the inscription cited by Dr. Hommel in support of the contrary view, the Museum of the Louvre possesses several similar ones discovered by M. de Sarzec at Telloh. If the text translated by Dr. Hommel does not come from Telloh, it must have been moved from its original place, like the tablet of black stone, with a Semitic inscription of Dungi, believed to have been found at Nineveh, and accordingly quoted by Dr. Hommel to show that the empire of the kings of Ur extended as far as that city. The text itself of the inscription, imperfectly copied by Lenormant, proves that its primitive resting-place was Cutha. [2] But yet more. Two princes of Shirpurla, Uru-Kagina in his barrel-inscription, and Gudea in the cylinder-inscription A, state that they have worked upon a canal, Ninâ-ki-tum-a, "the favourite river of the goddess Ninâ." In order to find this canal I believe it will be useless to ascend as far as the Khausser, the river of Nineveh, if we compare with the context these lines of M. de Sarzec: "In going from the Shatt-el-Haï to the ruins, at 500 metres from the *enceinte* of Telloh we meet with the bed of an immense canal, still visible, though filled with sand, running from N.W. to S.E. It is possibly the original channel of the Shatt-el-Haï, possibly also some canal derived from that great artery, and intended to supply the city with water." ₁

Uru-azagga and Gishgalla-ki still remain. The first must be sought near Telloh, if not in Telloh itself, since M. de Sarzec has found in the ruins: (1) at least one brick commemorating the erection by Gudea of a temple of the goddess Gatumdug situated in Uru-azagga; ₂ (2) the forepart of a lion or griffon of calcareous stone, which bears the same inscription as the brick of Gudea, some insignificant variants excepted; ₃ (3) a doorstep of the patesi Nammaghâni, intended for the temple of the goddess Bau, which the inscriptions on several statues of Gudea place in Uru-azagga; ₄ (4) a buttress of the patesi Entena intended for the temple of the goddess Gatumdug in Uru-azagga. ₅ As for Gishgalla-ki, which is known only from two passages in the inscription on the statue of Ur-Bau, one of-which calls the patesi "servant of the divine king of Gishgalla-ki," and the other places in Gishgalla-ki a temple of the goddess Ninni, its name even remains an obscure problem. It must have been some locality in Telloh or its immediate vicinity. Otherwise the inscription of Ur-Bau would offer us the only example in our texts of a foreign temple constructed by the princes of Shirpurla, and the sole example also of the title of "servant" of a foreign god assumed by one of them.

It will now be easy for me to show that the four centres, Girsu-ki, Uru-azagga, Ninâ-ki, and Gishgalla-ki, were only quarters. of a large city, which bore the name of Shirpurla-ki. Whenever the princes who have reigned at Telloh wished to indicate the whole of their capital or their domain, we shall see that they called it Shirpurla-ki. Only when they preferred to mark the extent of their domain by means of its extreme or most important points, or when they wanted to indicate a particular spot, they employed the names Girsu-ki, Uru-azagga, Ninâ-ki, and Gishgalla-ki.

It is thus that all call themselves "kings" or "patesis" of Shirpurla-ki. There is but one exception, and only in one of the three inscriptions he has left us; Uru-Kagina entitles himself on his cylinder "king of Girsu-ki." This exception can be easily explained, since Girsu-ki was without doubt the most important quarter of Shirpurla. It is thus again that Gudea, wishing to inform us what were the distant countries from which he derived the materials necessary for the buildings of his capital, expresses himself as follows: "By the power of Ninâ and Nin-girsu, to Gudea who holds his sceptre from

Nin-Girsu, the countries of Mâgan, Melughgha, Gubi, and Nituk, rich in trees of every species, have sent him at Shirpurla-ki ships laden with all sorts of trees" (statue D, col. 4). Thus, too, if I understand the passage rightly, after having enumerated the reforms which followed his accession to the throne, he describes the peace resulting therefrom to his country: "On the territory of Shirpurla-ki no one has sued him who has right on his side; a brigand has entered the house of no one" (statue B, col. 5).

But if the same Gudea wants to insist on the peace which he has given his country, and to prove that no part of his city was excluded from his care, he tells us: "Gudea, patesi of Shirpurla-ki, has proclaimed peace from Girsu-ki to Uru-azagga" (statue G, col. 2). So, too, in describing the position of a temple, the princes of Telloh never say that it was situated in Shirpurla, but more precisely in Girsu-ki, in Uru-azagga, in Ninâ-ki, or in Gishgalla-ki.

It is very difficult at present to determine the approximate situation in Telloh of these different quarters. I will, however, make some suggestions in regard to them.

The four *tels* or mounds on the west side of Telloh perhaps represent the site of Ninâ-ki. From one of them M. de Sarzec has recovered the beautiful bull and the tablet of black stone which bear the name of Dungi, and mention the erection of the temple of the goddess Ninâ. All the other *tels*, including the great *tel* on which stood the palace, appear to have formed part of Girsu-ki. It is in this region that bronzes and votive tablets have been discovered with the names of the god Nin-Girsu and of his sons Gal-alim and Dun-shagâna; now we cannot doubt, though we are not directly assured of it, that the temples of these three gods were situated in Girsu-ki. As for Uru-azagga, it is not certain that it lay in the part of Telloh excavated by M. de Sarzec. With the exception of some statues, which have certainly not been found. in their original position, the monuments intended, according to their inscriptions, for this quarter of Shirpurla-ki are little numerous; and some, if not all, appear to have been displaced, and, to use the expression of M. Heuzey, to have been replaced by the successive occupants of Telloh, which was still inhabited in the Parthian epoch. Nothing can be said concerning Gishgalla-ki, which is mentioned only on the statue of Ur-Bau.

II. We now possess the names of twelve or thirteen princes of Shirpurla, four or five of whom bear the title of "king," and eight the title of "patesi." M. Heuzey has shown by arguments derived from the more archaic character of their monuments and writing that the most ancient of these princes were the kings. He has also established that among the patesis the group comprising Entena and En-anna-tumma was the oldest. The script used by these patesis is still linear like that of the kings, and not yet cuneiform like that of the later princes. Of course I refer only to the inscriptions engraved on hard materials, bronze or stone. For we possess a clay cylinder of the king Uru-Kagina, where the wedge already appears as distinctly as on the bricks and cylinders of Gudea. We know that it is just by the form of the stylus employed by the scribes when writing upon soft clay that the wedge which characterises the cuneiform script is explained. It is by imitation only that it has passed from writing on clay to writing on stone.

The dynasties of Telloh were the following:

(1) Kings of Shirpurla-ki:—

The earliest king known is perhaps Ur-Ninâ, "the man of Ninâ," of whom we have three inscriptions. This prince was the son of a personage called Nini-ghal-gin (the reading Ghal-gin being uncertain). It is doubtful whether Nini-ghal-gin had himself been king, since his son never gives him the. title of sovereign.

After Ur-Ninâ, according to the "Stêlê of the Vultures," his son, A-Kurgal ("the son of Bel"?) reigned.

Another passage in the Stêlê of the Vultures appears to mention a certain Igi-ginna ("he who goes before") as king of Shirpurla.

So far as we can judge from the writing, it was after these monarchs that Uru-kagina reigned, ₁ whose three inscriptions have come down to us. Two of them call him "king of Shirpurla"; in a third, on a clay cylinder, he bears, as was first recognised by Dr. Oppert, the title of "king of Girsu-ki." ₂

(2) Patesis of Shirpurla-ki:—

The first series comprises three patesis, whose succession cannot at present be exactly determined. The museum of the Louvre possesses a portion of a buttress inscribed with the name of a patesi Entena, who does not record the name of his father, and another block bearing the name of a patesi En-anna-tumma, son of a patesi Entena. As the British Museum possesses a block inscribed by a patesi Entena, son of a patesi En-anna-tumma, we have a choice of two hypotheses. Either the patesi Entena of the British Museum is the same as the patesi Entena of the Louvre, in which case the succession will be: En-anna-tumma I, Entena, and En-anna-tumma II; or else the Entena of the British Museum is the grandson of that of the Louvre, the order of the patesis being Entena I, En-anna-tumma, Entena II.

Later in date than this family of princes comes the patesi Ur-Bau ("man of Bau") whose statue is in the Louvre, together with a number of monuments of less importance.

A short time after Ur-Bau comes Gudea ("the elect"), followed by his son and probable successor Ur-Nin-girsu ("man of Nin-girsu"). [1] It is of Gudea that the larger and more important part of the monuments of Telloh preserve the memory: eight statues, two large cylinders of clay, and hundreds of fragments or small texts. Of his successor we have a few bricks and a small object of uncertain use.

Here must be placed, I believe, the patesi Nammaghâni

("His supremacy") whose reign is assigned by Dr. Hommel to a period before Ur-Bau. But his monuments are too few (only a door-step and some bricks) to allow us to determine with certainty his relative date.

M. Heuzey has also made us acquainted with another patesi, Luka-ni ("His glory"). [1] His son Ghalalamma, who does not, like his father, take the title of patesi, offers homage in an inscription on the fragment of a statue to Dungi, king of Ur. [2]

It is difficult to determine, even approximately, to what remote epoch the dynasties of Telloh must be referred. We gather but little from the fact that the son of one of the last patesis of Shirpurla was the contemporary of Dungi. For we cannot yet fix the age of the early kings of Ur. Let me, however, hazard a hypothesis, in consideration of any light it may throw on the dark problem of Chaldean chronology.

I have already had occasion to cite an inscription of Gudea (on statue D) in which this patesi tells us that he received from "the countries of Mâgan, Melughgha, Gubi, and Nituk," vessels laden with all sorts of trees. The situation of Nituk is known. It was the Isle of Tilmun [3] in the Persian Gulf. It is not possible, in my opinion, to look for Mâgan and Melughgha anywhere else than in the vicinity of the Sinaitic Peninsula. Gubi, sometimes written Gubin, alone remains, which Dr. Hommel would identify with Byblos in Phœnicia, the Gapuna of the hieroglyphic texts. I should, however, prefer to see in Gubi a name of Egypt, and more precisely the name of Coptos, the ancient Qubti. Gudea would thus in his list of names have followed the route of his vessels, starting from the most distant points to the north of the Red Sea, coasting along Egypt and turning round Arabia. If the identification of Gubi or Gubin with Qubti meets with the approval of Egyptologists and Assyriologists, the reign of Gudea might perhaps be placed in the interval between the sixth Egyptian dynasty, when the monuments of Pepi seem already to testify to the commercial importance of Coptos, [2] and the eleventh, when the cities of Upper Egypt obtained political supremacy. No one of course will dream of bringing the reign of Gudea down to a later date.

How must we explain the fact that the last princes of Shirpurla contented themselves with the title of "patesi," while the most ancient took that of "king"? I believe that it is difficult not to see in this fact an indication of the loss of its earlier independence on the part of Shirpurla and of its subjection to some other city, probably Ur. All the other instances we have of the use of the title of "patesi," lend it the sense of "lieutenant" before the name of a country, of "vicar" before a divine name. ₁ We possess inscriptions in which the patesis of Nipur and of Ishkun-Sin acknowledge their dependency on the kings of Ur. Nebuchadnezzar II calls himself the patesi of the god Merodach, Sargon the patesi of the god Assur. The title of the earliest sovereigns of Assyria, "patesi of the god Assur," defines their power as being that either of a kingdom predominantly religious, or of a viceroyalty under a suzerain, who was without doubt Babylonian. It always implies the idea of lieutenant or dependant. Why should we admit an exception in the case of Shirpurla? It is true that Gudea comes before us as a powerful prince. In one of his inscriptions (statue B) he boasts of having overthrown the city of Anshan in the land of Elam. But for aught we know he may have made this expedition in the company of his suzerain. Dependence, moreover, admits of degrees, and it can even be purely nominal. France has known powerful vassals who have resisted royalty.

III. The campaign of Gudea in Elam, in the course of which the city of Anshan was captured, is the only fact of military history of which we know. We have a little better information, thanks to two inscriptions of the same patesi (those of statue B and cylinder A), concerning the commercial relations of his country. Unfortunately it is always very difficult to identify the geographical names recorded in the texts.

From a passage cited above it appears that Shirpurla enjoyed commercial intercourse with the countries of Nituk, Gubi or Gubin, Mâgan, and Melughgha. These four countries furnished Chaldæa with wood for building. But Melughgha also furnished gold, and Mâgan a hard stone, diorite, which was employed by the sculptors. Chaldæa was also in connection with the country of Martu, that is to say, with Phœnicia and Syria. From a mountain which seems to have been Amanus, it derived cedars and other trees; from two other mountains of Martu—Susalla and Tidanum ₁—two species of stones. It is stones again that were imported from a mountain of Barsip, which I should look for in the neighbourhood of the Syrian city of Til-Barsip. For I believe that it is the same country as that which appears in W.A.I., ii. 53, *a* 3, under the varying forms of Barsip-ki and Bursip-ki. We know that the name of Til-Barsip was also written Til-Bursip. The inscription of statue B, moreover, tells us that the stones coming from Barsip were conveyed in vessels which, according to my view, would have had only to descend the Euphrates. I am greatly tempted to ascend still farther to the north, towards the sources of this river, in order to find two other countries—

the city of Ursu-ki, in the mountains of Ibla (or rather, Tilla ₁), which furnished wood, and Shamalum, or Shamanum, in the mountains of Menua, which furnished stones. But I can suggest nothing in regard to three other geographical names which I shall confine myself to mentioning: the mountain of Ghaghum, from whence Gudea procured gold; the city of Abullat or Abulla-Abishu ("the great gate of his fathers"), situated in the mountains of Ki-mash, 2 whence he procured copper; and the country or city of Madga, in the mountains of the river Gurruda (?), 3 from whence he procured a product whose precise nature I am unable to determine.

Certain cities of Babylonia are mentioned in our texts. They are the three ancient cities of Eridu (*Nun-ki*), Larrak (*Barbar-ki*), and the unknown city of Kinunir-ki. They always appear to figure as sacred cities, and the last of the three only after the name of a goddess, Duzi-abzu, "the mistress of Kinunir."

The names of the Euphrates and Tigris frequently occur on the two cylinders of Gudea. I believe I have also found in them the names of Shumer and Accad— "Kiengi" and "Ki-burbur." But it is not yet possible for me to translate the passages where they are found.

The inscription of statue B mentions two seas. "After he had caused the temple of Nin-girsu to be built, Nin-girsu, the lord beloved by him, has forcibly opened for him the roads from the sea of the highlands to the lower sea." The "sea of the highlands " is evidently the Persian Gulf, and it is impossible to doubt that by the "lower sea" is intended the Mediterranean.

IV. For a knowledge of the pantheon of Shirpurla-ki we possess a document of a very great value. This is the list of divinities at the commencement of the imprecatory formula in the inscription on statue B of Gudea. The following are the names of the divinities, which it is important to give in the order, evidently sacred, in which they are enumerated in the inscription:—

Anna, the Sky-god, the Anu of the Semites; Ellilla or Bel, "the lord of the mountain of the world," 1 where the seat of the gods was placed, as well as the habitation of the dead, also called "the father of the gods;" Nin-gharsag or Belit, "the mistress of the mountain," the wife of Ellilla, and mother of the gods; En-ki or Ea, "the lord of the earth" and the waters;

En-zu, or Sin, the Moon-god, the eldest son of Ellilla; Nin-girsu or Ninib, the Chaldean Hercules, the son and warrior of Ellilla; Ninâ, the daughter of Ea, who has the same titles as Nin-dara, and may therefore be regarded as the consort of this god; Nin-dara, who is the god Ninib 1 under another name; Gatumdug, the daughter of Anna, who is the goddess Bau under another name; Bau, daughter of Anna and wife of Nin-girsu; Ninni or Nanâ, the Ishtar of the Semites, another daughter of Anna; Shamash, the Sun-god, the son of En-ki or Ea; Pasagga, the Ishum of the Semites, who is undoubtedly only another form of Gibil, the Fire-god, the son of En-id or Ea;

Gal-alim, the son of Nin-girsu; Dun-shagâna, another son of Nin-girsu; Nin-mar-ki, the eldest daughter of Nina;

Duzi-abzu, "lady of Kinunir-ki;" Nin-gish-zida, the god of Gudea.

It will be observed that this list arranges the divinities in three generations. In the first come the four great gods, including a goddess, distinguished also by the later Assyro-Babylonian religious systems, and from whom all the other gods proceed. Next are placed the sons and daughters of these deities. Lastly come the grandchildren. I have been obliged to put Duzi-abzu and Nin-gish-zida by themselves, since no text has as yet given us any information concerning them. ₂ But we may believe that one of them—Nin-gish-zida—must be mentioned at the end of the list, whatever may have been his rank in the divine family, since, as we shall see, he was the special deity of Gudea and his intercessor with the other gods.

The preceding list does not give all the gods mentioned in the texts of Telloh; some even are absent who had their temples in Shirpurla. Without pretending to be complete, I may further enumerate the god Nin-âgal, who is only another form of En-ki; the god Shidlamta-êna, another name of Nin-girsu, and the Nergal of the Semites; the god Nin-sar, yet another name of Nergal; the goddess Nin-tu, another designation of Nin-gharsag; the god Uru-ki or Sin; the god Nirba; perhaps the god Nin-shagh, Pap-sukal; a god called the "king" of Gishgalla-ki; a goddess Kû-anna; a god Dun-sir (?)-anna; seven sons of Bau, who are termed Zazaru (or Zazauru), Im-ghud-êna, Ur-un-ta-êna (or Gim-nun-ta-êna), Ghi-gir-nunna, Ghi-shaga, Gurmu, and Zarmu.

In a learned article in the *Zeitschrift für Assyriologie* (ii. pp. 179 *seq.*), Prof. Tiele has shown that at Babylon, by the side of the local god Bel-Merodach and even in his temple of Ê-shagil, his wife and son Zarpanit and Nebo were also adored; that at Borsippa, by the side of the supreme god Nebo and in his temple of Ê-Zida, his consort Nanâ was worshipped. If we remember that other temples existed at Babylon dedicated to various other deities, we shall readily admit that the cult rendered to these gods was offered by reason of their being the mother, the brothers, or the sisters of the principal divinity. We may remark, moreover, that the supreme god of the national or local pantheon was hardly ever one of the primordial deities. The latter, indeed, appear to me to have been born after their sons, in consequence of the need experienced by the mind of man to establish for his god a family analogous to his own, with parents, wife, and children. The two exceptions which may be instanced from Nipur and Eridu are not certain. Dr. Hommel has remarked that one text at all events names Ninib and not Bel as the chief divinity of Nipur. As for Eridu, I do not feel sure that the principal deity there was really Ea. This god had certainly a temple in Eridu, just as he had at Shirpurla-ki, but in both cities it was under the title of the divine father that he was adored. The very interesting inscription on a brick of a patesi of Eridu, named Idadu, which is unfortunately still unpublished, would lead us to suppose that the chief god of the place was Nin-Eridu, possibly a name of Merodach. ₁

The supreme god of Shirpurla was Nin-girsu, whose consort was the goddess Bau. Both were worshipped under different titles. Besides the temples in which he was invoked as Nin-girsu, he had others in Girsu-ki, where he was known as Nin-dara and Shidlamta-êna. Similarly the goddess was not only adored as Bau, but she was also worshipped in Uru-azagga as Gatumdug and in Ninâ-ki as Ninâ. Three at least of the parent gods had sanctuaries in Shirpurla,— Ellilla (called specially "the father of Nin-girsu"), En-ki, and "the mother of the gods," Nin-gharsag. Temples were even dedicated to En-ki under his two titles of En-ki and Nin-âgal. We may question whether it was in virtue of her being his wife or his sister that Ninni possessed a temple in Girsu-ki and another in Gishgalla-ki; and also whether Nin-gish-zida, in his special temple at Girsu-ki, was worshipped as being a brother of the god or as being the god himself under a fourth manifestation. It is certain, on the other hand, that Gal-alim and Dun-shâgana had each a temple because they were the sons of Nin-girsu, and that Nin-mar-ki had one because she was the daughter of Ninâ. We do not know at present what were the grounds of relationship which caused temples to be erected in Girsu-ki to the goddesses Kû-anna ₁ and Duzi-abzu. It is possible that some of these numerous temples were only chapels situated in Ê-ninnû, the favourite sanctuary of Nin-girsu; those, for example, which belonged to the sons of the god.

While regarding Nin-girsu as the supreme object of his cult, as "his king," to use the stereotyped expression, each prince of Shirpurla-lei selected also a special deity from among the divine family, who acted as his intercessor with Nin-girsu. ₂ We are acquainted with the deities of five of these princes. That of Uru-Kagina was perhaps Nin-shagh or Pap-sukal—though the reading is doubtful; that of Entena and En-anna-tumma was Dun-sir(?)-anna; that of Ur-Bau was Nin-âgal; that of Gudea, Nin-gish-zida.

We have not yet succeeded in ascertaining the exact sense of the various appellations of Nin-girsu and his wife Bau; it is consequently impossible to define with precision the character and personality of these divinities. We may admit, however, that Nin-girsu was a solar deity, personifying more particularly the sun when veiled in clouds; hence the combative and military aspect of the god. Like Apollo, with whom he would be more fitly compared than with Hercules, he was at once an avenger and a saviour, a huntsman, and perhaps a shepherd. As for Bau, who was termed "the mother" *par excellence*, and to whom were given the titles of "good lady," "Mistress of Abundance," she was a terrestrial divinity, resembling in many points the Demeter of the Greeks. It is even possible that like Demeter she presided also over Hades, and not only over the living and fertile earth. Two of our texts mention a festival of Bau, which occurred, if I understand the passage aright, at the commencement of the year;

and it appears to result from another inscription that the chief festival of Nin-girsu took place at the same time. Indeed it is probable that it was at the beginning of the year, at the vernal equinox, that the cities of Babylonia and Assyria alike celebrated the festivals of their gods.

The following translations comprise almost all the texts hitherto brought from Telloh, with the exception of the inscription on the so-called Stélé of the Vultures and those on the two large cylinders of Gudea.

Restorations of the text are indicated by brackets—[]. Words placed in parentheses—()—have been added in order to render the sense more intelligible.

Certain of the inscriptions have been published in *Découvertes en Chaldée*, par E. de Sarzec, edited by L. Heuzey, of which the first two parts have appeared in 1884 and 1887.

Footnotes

42:1 See also M. Léon Heuzey's *Un Palais Chaldéen* (Paris, Leroux, 1888).

42:2 On all these points, see Hommel's *Geschichte Babyloniens and Assyriens* (Berlin, 1885-87).

43:1 According to Mr. Pinches (*Guide to the Kouyunjik Gallery*, London, 1885, p. 7, note 2), Shir-pur-la-ki would be an ideographic mode of writing the word Lagash. We should then perhaps have to compare W.A.I., ii. 52, *a* 60, which seems to connect a city Lagashu-ki with Urama or "Ur" (?).

45:1 The pronunciation of the name of the goddess Ninâ and of the city called after her is still problematical.

45:2 See the Zeitschrift für Assyriologie, iii., p. 94.

46:1 *Découvertes en Chaldée*, p. 12.

46:2 Not yet published.

46:3 I owe my knowledge of this fact, as well as of several others, to the kindness of M. Heuzey.

46:4 *Découvertes en Chaldée*, pl. 27, 1.

46:5 Not yet published.

50:1 See Heuzey: "Un nouveau roi de Tello," in the *Revue Archéologique* of 1884.

50:2 It would seem that a prince more ancient than Uru-Kagina and perhaps as ancient as Ur-Ninâ bore the title of "patesi" and not of "king." But his name still remains unknown. See below, p. 67.

51:1 Cf. Ledrain: *Communication à l'Académie des Inscriptions et Belles-Lettres*, 12th July 1882.

52:1 "Le Roi Dounghi" in the *Revue Archéologique*, April 1886.

52:2 I omit a patesi of Shirpurla, En-anna, made known to us by George Smith in his *Early History of Babylonia*, and two other patesis whose names are quoted by Dr. Hommel from some seals (*Geschichte Bab. und Ass.*, pp. 290, 293). The text translated by George Smith has not yet been published, and the reading of the inscriptions on the seals does not seem absolutely certain.

52:3 [Identified with the Tylos of classical geography by Dr. Oppert, and with the modern Bahrein by Sir H. Rawlinson, though Professor Delitzsch considers it to form part of the delta which has accumulated at the mouth of the Euphrates.— *Ed.*]

53:1 This is the opinion long ago maintained by Messrs. Lenormant, Oppert, and Sayce. M. Delattre has ably defended it in the memoir *L'Asie occidentale dans les Inscriptions Assyriennes*, pp. 149 Seq.

53:2 See Maspero: *Histoire ancienne* (4th edit.), p. 81.

54:1 [I should rather render it "High-Priest." See my *Lectures on the Religion of the Ancient Babylonians*, pp. 59-60.— *Ed.*]

55:1 The reading Susalla is uncertain. Dr. Hommel has compared Tidanum with Tidnu, the Sumerian equivalent of Akharru (the Semitic term for Syria).

56:1 Dr. Hommel has proposed to read Dalla.

56:2 [Ki-mash seems to be "the country of Mas," or Arabia Petræa; comp. the Mash of Genesis x. 23. The Babylonians derived a name for "copper," *kemassu*, from its Sumerian appellation.— *Ed.*

56:3 Can the river Gurruda have been the Dead Sea, and can the product derived from the neighbouring district have been bitumen, as Dr. Hommel has conjectured? It is not probable that all the bitumen required for the buildings of Babylonia was exclusively provided by the little river of Hit. (See Hdt. i. 199.)

57:1 In an abbreviated form, "the lord of the world."

58:1 [Or Uras.— *Ed.*]

58:2 If our Duzi-abzu is a goddess—and her title of "lady of Kinunir-ki" does not allow us to doubt it—it is clear that we cannot identify her with the god Duzi-abzu who is named in W.A.I., ii. 56, 33-38, as one of the six sons of Ea. It is necessary to understand six sons in this passage, and not six children, since the following line names "a daughter" of Ea.

60:1 See George Smith in the *Transactions of the Society of Biblical Archæology*, i. p. 32.

61:1 Consort of the god Martu, according to the *Collection de Clercq*, cyl. 114. Cf. W.A.I., iii. 67, *b* 35.

61:2 See more especially the last lines of inscription No. 1 of King Uru-Kagina. M. Heuzey has drawn my attention to the lines, which have been translated for the first time by Dr. Oppert.

I. The Inscriptions of King Ur-Nina

No. 1. ɪ—COLUMN I

1. Ninâ-ur

2. king

3. of SHIRPURLA,

4. son of Nini-ghal-gin,

5. the temple of the god NIN-GIRSU

6. has erected.

7. The *Ib-gal* (?)

8. he has erected.

9. The temple of the goddess NINÂ

10. he has erected.

COLUMN II

1. The *Sig-nir* (?)

2. he has erected.

3. His tower in stages (?)

4. he has erected.

5. The temple of Ê ...

6. he has erected.

7. The temple of Ê-GHUD

8. he has erected.

9. His observatory (?)

10. he has erected.

COLUMN III

? [The palace]

1. of the *Ti-ash-ra* (?)

2. he has erected.

3. The temple of the goddess GATUMDUG

4. he has erected.

5. The great *apzu* ₁

6. he has constructed.

7. After that the temple of NIN-GIRSU

8. he has caused to be erected

9. seventy great *measures* (?) of corn

10. in his house of fruits

COLUMN IV

? [he has stored up.]

1. From MÂGAN 2

2. the mountain 3

3. all sorts of wood he has imported.

4. The castle 4 of SHIRPURLA

5. he has built.

6. The small *apzu*

7. he has constructed;

COLUMN V

? [in the temple]

1. of the goddess NINÂ, lady of destinies (?),

2. he has placed it.

3. Two statues (?)

4. he has set up (?);

5. these two statues (?) …

. . . .

Lacuna.

No. 2. 1—COLUMN I

1. Ninâ-ur

2. the king

3. of SHIRPURLA,

4. son of Nini-ghal-gin,

5. the *habitation* (?) of GIRSU

COLUMN II

1. has constructed.

2. The bricks of the foundation (?)

....

The inscription breaks of here.

_____

No. 3. 2—COLUMN I

1. Ninâ-ur

2. the king

3. of SHIRPURLA,

COLUMN II

1. the son of Nini-ghal-g[in].

Footnotes

64:1 *Découvertes en Chaldée*, pl. 2, No. 1. Translated by Dr, Oppert in a *Communication to the Académie des Inscriptions et Belles-Lettres*, 2d March 1883.

65:1 [The *apzu*, or "deep," was the basin for purification attached to a Babylonian temple, corresponding to the "sea" of Solomon.— *Ed.*]

65:2 The Sinaitic Peninsula, perhaps including Midian.

65:3 Or "the country."

65:4 Or "wall."

66:1 *Découvertes*, pl. 2, No. 2. Translated by Dr. Hommel, *Geschichte Babyloniens und Assyriens*, p. 285.

66:2 L. Heuzey, "Les Rois de Tello," in the *Revue Archéologique*, Nov. 1882.

II. Inscription of an Unknown Prince on a Boulder of Stone [1]

COLUMN I

Lacuna.

1. [pate]si

2. [of SHIRPUR]LA

....

COLUMN II

1. [of the god] NIN-GIRSU

2. [the...] *dun*

3. has constructed.

4. The palace of *Ti-ra-ash-di* (?)

5. he has built,

6. and he has...

7. E-an-[na]-du [2]

8. covered with renown

COLUMN III

1. by the god NIN-GIRSU,

2. for the countries

3. by the power of the god NIN-GIRSU

. . . .

The last lines are destroyed.

Footnotes

67:1 Découvertes, pl. 2, No. 3. The writing used in this inscription resembles that of the inscriptions of Ur-ninâ and the Stêlê of the Vultures more than any other. However, the little that remains of the first column seems to indicate that it belongs to a patesi and not to a king, perhaps to an E-anna-du.

67:2 This proper name is mutilated, but I believe my reading very probable. Cf. the Stêlê of the Vultures, Obv. i. 1.

III. Inscriptions of Uru-Kagina

No. 1. 1—COLUMN I

1. For the god NIN-GIRSU

2. the warrior of the god ELLILLA,

3. Uru-Kagina,

4. the king

5. of SHIRPURLA-KI,

6. his temple

7. has constructed.

8. His palace of Ti-ra-ash

9. he has constructed.

COLUMN II

1. The *an-ta-shur-ra*

2. he has constructed.

3. The *E-gish-me-ra*

4. in order to [be] the *E-ne-bi* of the countries

5. he has constructed.

6. The house of fruits which produces abundance (?) in the country

7. he has constructed.

8. For the god DUN-SHAGÂNA

9. his habitation of AKKIL

COLUMN III

1. he has constructed.

2. For the god GAL-ALIMMA

3. the temple of E-ME-GAL-GHUSH-AN-KI

4. he has constructed.

5. The temple of the goddess BAU ₁

6. he has constructed.

7. For the god ELLILLA

8. the temple of E-ADDA, ₂

9. his *im-sag-ga,*

COLUMN IV

1. he has constructed.

2. The *Bur* (?)- *sag,*

3. his temple which rises to the entrance of heaven (?),

4. he has constructed.

5. Of Uru-Kagina,

6. the king

7. of SHIRPURLA-KI,

8. who the temple of E-NINNÙ

9. has constructed,

10. his god

COLUMN V

1. is the god NIN-SHAGH. ₃

2. For the life of the king

3. during the long days to come

4. before the god NIN-GIRSU

5. may he (NIN-SHAGH) bow down his face!

———————

No. 2—ON A BUTTRESS

1. [For the god NIN-GIRSU],

2. [the] warrior

3. [of the god EL]LILLA,

4. [Uru-]Ka[g]ina,

5. [the] king

6. [of SHIRPUR]LA-KI,

7. [the *Anta*]- *Shurra*,

8. [the house] of abundance of his country,

9. [has] constructed.

10. His [palace] of Ti-[ra-ash]

11. [he] has constructed.

Lines 12 *and* 13 *are destroyed.*

14. [For the god] GAL-ALIMMA

Line s 15–21 *are destroyed.*

22. [he has] constructed.

23. [For the god] NIN-SAR,

24. the bearer [of the sword?]

25. [of the god] NIN-GIRSU,

26. his temple

27. he has constructed.

28. [For the god …] GIR (?)

29. the well-beloved

30. [of the god] NIN-GIRSU

31. his temple

32. he has constructed.

33. The *Bur* (?)- *sag,*

34. his temple which rises to the entrance of heaven (?),

35. he has constructed.

36. For the god ELLILLA

37. the temple of E-ADDA?, 1

38. HIS *IM-SAG-GA*,

39. HE HAS CONSTRUCTED.

40. FOR THE GOD NIN-GIRSU

41. THE *SANCTUARY* (?)

42. OF E-MELAM-KURRA 2

43. HE HAS CONSTRUCTED.

44. THE TEMPLE WHEREIN *DWELLS* (?) THE GOD NIN-GIRSU

45. HE HAS CONSTRUCTED.

46. OF URU-KAGINA,

47. who the temple

48. of the god NIN-GIRSU …

The inscription breaks of here, having never been finished.

No. 3.—ON A CYLINDER 1

COLUMN I

The first lines are lost.

1. Uru-Kagina,

2. the king

3. Of GIRSU-KI,

4. the *Anta-shurra*,

5. the house of abundance of his country,

6. his palace of TI-RA-ASH,

7. has constructed.

8. The temple of the goddess BAU

9. [he has] constructed.

Lacuna.

COLUMN II

The first lines are lost.

1. he has [constructed].

2. For the god [DUN-SHA]GA[NA]

3. his habitation of [AKKIL]

4. he has [constructed].

5. For the god ...

6. his tablet-like amulets (?) ₂

7. (and) his temple he has made.

8. In the middle (of this temple)

9. for the god ZA-ZA-URU,

10. for the god IM-GHUD-ÊN,

11. for the god GIM-NUN-TA-ÊN-A

12. temples he has built for them.

13. For the god NIN-SAR

Lacuna.

COLUMN III

The first lines are lost.

1. [For the god ELLIL]LA

2. [the temple of E-]ADDA, his [*im* -] *sagga,*

3. he has constructed.

4. For the goddess NINÂ,

5. her favourite river,

6. the canal NINÂ-KI-TUM-A

7. he has *excavated* (?).

8. At the mouth (of the canal), an edifice...

Fragments of four other columns remain.

Footnotes

68:1 From a squeeze in the Louvre. Translated by Dr. Oppert in a *Communication to the Académie des Inscriptions*, 29th February 1884.

69:1 [Bau is probably the Baau of Phœnician mythology, whose name was interpreted "the night," and who was supposed along with her husband Kolpia, "the wind," to have produced the first generation of men. The word has been compared with the Hebrew *bohu,* translated "void" in Gen. i. 2.—Ed.]

69:2 ["The temple of the father."— *Ed.*]

69:3 Or Nin-dun.

70:1 ["The temple of the father."— *Ed.*]

70:2 ["The temple of the brilliance of the (eastern) mountain."— *Ed.*]

71:1 *Découvertes,* pl. 32.

71:2 Possibly the small tablets of white or black stone buried under the foundations of the temples. These tablets were sometimes of metal; those, for example, discovered at

Khorsabad. It seems that some consisted also of ivory and precious wood; see W.A.I., i. 49, col. 4, 12.

IV. Inscription of Entena on a Buttress

1. To the goddess GATUMDUG,

2. the mother of SHIRPURLA-KI,

3. Entena,

4. the patesi

5. of SHIRPURLA-KI,

6. who has built the temple of the goddess GATUMDUG.

7. His god

8. is the god DUN-SIR(?)-ANNA.

V. Inscription of En-anna-tumma on a Buttress [1]

1. For the god NIN-GIRSU,

2. the warrior of the god ELLILLA,

3. En-anna-tumma,

4. the patesi

5. Of SHIRPURLA-KI,

6. the chosen of the heart

7. of the goddess NINÂ,

8. the great patesi

9. of the god NIN-GIRSU,

10. the son of Entena

11. the patesi

12. of SHIRPURLA-KI.

13. For the god NIN-GIRSU

14. his house of fruits

15. he has restored.

16. Of En-anna-tumma,

17. who the house of fruits

18. of the god NIN-GIRSU

19. has restored,

20. his god

21. is the god DUN-SIR(?)-ANNA.

Footnotes

74:1 *Découvertes*, pl. 6, No. 4.

VI. Inscriptions of Ur-Bau and his Reign

No. I.—ON A STATUE 1

COLUMN I

1. To the god NIN-GIRSU

2. the powerful warrior

3. of the god ELLILLA,

4. Ur-Bau

5. the patesi

6. of SHIRPURLA-KI,

7. the offspring begotten

8. by the god NIN-ÂGAL,

9. chosen by the immutable will of the goddess NINÁ,

10. endowed with power by the god NIN-GIRSU,

11. named with a favourable name by the goddess BAU,

12. endowed with intelligence by the god EN-KI, 2

COLUMN II

1. covered with renown by the goddess NINNI,

2. the favourite servant of the god who is king of GISHGALLA-KI,

3. the favourite of the goddess DUZI-ABZU.

4. I am UR-BAU;

5. the god NIN-GIRSU is my king.

6. The site of ... 3 he has excavated.

7. The earth thence extracted, like precious stones, he has measured (?);

8. like a precious metal he has weighed (?) it.

COLUMN III

1. According to the plan adopted he has marked out a large space;

2. into the middle (of it) he has carried this earth,

3. and he has made its *mundus*. 1

4. Above, a substructure 6 cubits high, he has built.

5. Above this substructure

6. the temple E-NINNÛ, which illumines the darkness (?), 30 cubits in height,

7. he has built.

8. For the goddess NIN-GHARSAG, 2 the mother of the gods,

COLUMN IV

1. her temple of GIRSU-KI

2. he has constructed.

3. For the goddess BAU,

4. the good lady,

5. the daughter of ANNA,

6. her temple of URU-AZAGGA

7. he has constructed.

8. For the goddess NINNI, the lady august, the *sovereign* (?),

9. her temple of GISHGALLA-KI

10. he has constructed.

11. For the god EN-KI, the king of ERIDU,

12. his temple of GIRSU-KI

COLUMN V

1. he has constructed.

2. For the god NIN-DARA, 3 the lord of *destinies* (?),

3. his temple he has constructed.

4. For the god NIN-ÂGAL,

5. his god,

6. his temple

7. he has constructed.

8. For the goddess NIN-MAR-KI 1

9. the good lady,

10. the eldest daughter of the goddess NINÁ,

11. the *Esh-gu-tur* (?), the temple of her constant choice,

12. he has constructed.

COLUMN VI

1. For the god …

2. the shepherd … [of] GIR-[SU-KI],

3. his temple …

4. he has constructed.

5. For the goddess KÛ-ANNA, 2

6. the lady of the cloudy sky (?),

7. her temple of GIRSU-KI

8. he has constructed.

9. For the goddess DUZI-ABZU,

10. the lady of KINUNIR-KI,

11. her temple of GIRSU-KI

12. he has constructed.

The remaining inscriptions of Telloh will be translated in the next volume.

Footnotes

75:1 *Découvertes*, pll. 7 and 8. Translated by Dr. Oppert in a *Communication to the Académie des Inscriptions*, 31st March 1882.

75:2 [Also called Ea, the god of the deep.—Ed.]

75:3 Perhaps some edifice previously dedicated to the goddess Bau. The characters are destroyed.

76:1 This translation of these six lines is given under reserve. Should we compare the ceremonies at the foundation of cities in classical antiquity?

76:2 ["The lady of the mountain."— *Ed.*]

76:3 [Or Uras.— *Ed.*]

77:1 ["The lady of the city of Mar."— *Ed.*]

77:2 The consort of the god Martu [or Rimmon], according to a cylinder belonging to M. de Clercq (No. 114); cf. W.A.I., iii. 67, *b*. 35.

SIN-GASHID'S ENDOWMENT OF THE TEMPLE Ê-ANA

Translated by Theo. G. Pinches

THIS short inscription of twenty-seven lines is one of peculiar interest. It is a record, written in the Akkadian language, of an endowment, made by an early Mesopotamian king with a Semitic Babylonian name, to the great temple at Erech called Ê-ana; 1 and it is not an original, but a copy in clay, written by a man named Nabû-baladhsu-igbî, of a stone tablet kept, in ancient times, in the great temple known as Ê-zida, now the ruin called the Birs-i-Nimroud—the supposed tower of Babel. Great care has been taken by the copyist in inscribing the tablet; and the forms of the characters, as he has given them, probably reproduce fairly well the archaic style of the original. The text itself covers the greater part of the two sides of the clay tablet, which is, like most of the documents of this kind found in Babylonia and Assyria, flat—or nearly so—on the obverse, and curved on the reverse. The last three lines, which are separate from the others, are written smaller, and are in the later Babylonian style of writing. Unlike the rest, also, they are written in the Semitic-Babylonian language. The size of the tablet is 4¼ inches by 2⅜ inches, the thickness in the thickest part being 1⅛ inch. The colour is a very light yellow ochre.

As the word-order in Akkadian differs considerably from English, no attempt is made to preserve the divisions of the lines of the original; by this arrangement translations from these ancient tongues are much more easily understood.

TRANSLATION OF THE INSCRIPTION OF SIN-GASHID

Sin-gashid, 1 king of ERECH, 2 king of AMNANUM, and patron 3 ofÊ-ANA, to LUGAL-BANDA his god and NIN-GUL his goddess. When he built Ê-ANA he erected Ê-KANKAL, the house which is the seat of the joy of his heart. 4 During his dominion he will endow it with 5 30 *gur* of wheat, 12 *mana* of wool, 10 *mana* of produce, 18 *qa* of oil according to 6 the tariff, and 1 shekel of gold. May his years be years of plenty.

COLOPHON IN SEMITIC-BABYLONIAN:

Copy of the tablet of *ûsû* -stone, the property 7of Ê-ZIDA, which Nabû-baladhsu-igbî, son of Mitsirâa, 8 has written.

It may not be without interest to give here a transcription of the original text into Roman characters, omitting the determinative prefixes, which were probably not pronounced:—

Lugal-banda, dingiranir, Nin-gul amānir, Sin gashid, lugal Unuga, lugal Amnanum, ua Ê-ana. Ud Ê-ana mu-dua, Ê-kankal, ê ki-tur shaghulakanē, munen-du. Bala nam-lugalakani ba she-gur-ta, ghu-min mana sig-ta, ghu mana urn-ta (ghu-ussa-qa 1) salgish-ta, kilama dana-ka, guskin gi gê ghipdazig. Mua-ni mu ghigala ghia.

Gabri narua sha ûshî, nigga Ê-zida, Nabû-baladhsu-igbî, âbil Mitsirâa, isdhur.

The text begins with an invocation to Lugalbanda and his consort Nin-gul, who seem to have been Sin-gashid's patron god and goddess. He then speaks of Ê-ana, one of the great temples of Erech (which was, perhaps, Sin-gashid's capital), and Ê-kankal, probably one of the shrines in Ê-ana. Judging from the wording, Sin-gashid seems to claim to be the founder of both those fanes, though it is probable that he only rebuilt them. Sin-gashid then gives a list of the amounts of produce, etc., with which he had endowed the shrine, and ends with a pious wish for his country. The date of the original of this inscription may be set down at about 2600 B.C. The copy which has come down to us, however, probably dates from the time of the antiquarian revival in Babylonia during the reign of Nabonidus, father of Belshazzar.

It is to be noted that the inscription is dedicated to a god and a goddess whose names I provisionally transcribe as *Lugal-banda* ("powerful king," or "king of youthful strength") and *Nin-gul* his consort (as we learn from the second volume of the *Cuneiform Inscriptions of Western Asia*, pl. 59, ll. 24 and 25 ₁). This identification of Ningul as the consort of Lugal-banda is important, as it shows that Sin-gashid, who calls her his mother, and himself her son, ₂ did not mean to imply that she was his real earthly parent, but that he simply traced his descent from her, thus asserting his divine origin. The late George Smith's double-queried "Belat-sunat" (as he transcribed the name Nin-gul), "the earliest known queen in the Euphrates valley," must therefore be erased from the list of historical rulers in Erech.

The temple Ê-ana was probably the principal fane in the city of Erech, and Ê-kankal ₃ was probably one of the shrines within it. It is not improbable that the Ê-kankal mentioned here is the same as, or the fellow-shrine to, the Ê-ghili-ana mentioned by Assur-bani-pal as the sanctuary, apparently in or connected with Ê-ana, to which he restored the image of the goddess Nanâ, which was carried off by the king of Elam, Kudur-nankhundi, about 2280 years before Christ. As the date of Sin-gashid is doubtful, ₁ it is impossible to say with certainty whether the capture of the image of Nanâ by the Elamites took place before or after his reign, but it was probably after. ₂

The inscription here translated and explained is a duplicate of one published in the fourth volume of the *Cuneiform Ins. of W. Asia*, pl. 35, No. 3, from two cones from Warka. ₃ Of this text, which is rather roughly written, and which gives a few interesting variants from the text translated above, a tentative translation was given by the late George Smith in his "Early History of Babylonia," published in the *Transactions of the Society of Biblical Archæology*, vol. i., and in the first series of the Records of the Past, vol. iii.

Footnotes

78:1 Written *Ê-an-na* in the inscriptions. The end-syllable *-na* is, however, generally regarded as a kind of phonetic complement, and the n is therefore not really double. The name means "House of heaven."

80:1 This name is probably for *Sin-kashid*, "the Moon-god has made captive."

80:2 The Akkadian form is *Unuga*.

80:3 Literally "nourisher" (*ua*, equivalent to the Semitic-Babylonian *zaninu*).

80:4 The Akkadians here use the compound *sha-ghulla*, "heartjoy."

80:5 Literally, "measure out to it."

80:6 Or, perhaps, "according to the tariff of the time."

80:7 The original has the Akkadian word *nigga* = Semitic-Babylonian *mimma*.

80:8 Mitsirâa, "the Egyptian."

81:1 This is represented on the tablet by a single character formed with four wedges (three horizontal and one upright) of the same form as the character aš. This character is equivalent to 3×6 (= 18) *qa*.

82:1 From a comparison of the other names in the text there published, it would seem that other possible readings of these two names are *Umun-banda* or *Ûn-banda* and *Ûn-gul* or *Ê-gul*. Fresh excavations in the East can alone determine these points.

82:2 *Cun. Ins. of W. Asia*, vol. i. pl. 3, No. viii. (Brick from the summit of the Bowarieh ruin at Warka).

82:3 "The house of the sanctuary" (?).

83:1 He may be regarded as having reigned about 2600 B.C.

83:2 The text of Assur-bani-pal's description is as follows:—"For 1635 years had the goddess Nanā been angry, had gone, and had dwelt within Elam, which was not her proper place; and in those days she and the gods her fathers proclaimed my name to the dominion of the world. She intrusted to me the return of her divinity thus: 'Assur-bani-pal shall bring me out of the midst of wicked Elam, and shall cause me to enter within Ê-ana.' The words of the command of her divinity, which she had spoken from remote days, she again revealed to the later people. I grasped the hand of her great divinity, and she took the straight road, with joy of heart, to Ê-ana. In the month Kisleu, on the first day, I caused her to enter Erech, and in Ê-ghili-ana, which she loves, I caused an everlasting shrine to be founded for her."

83:3 The ancient Erech, in which the temple Ê-ana was situated.

AN ERECHITE'S LAMENT

TRANSLATED BY THEO. G. PINCHES

IN connection with the text referring to Ê-ana in Erech, the following, a kind of penitential psalm written in the Sumerian dialect, with a translation into Semitic-

Babylonian, which I have entitled "The Erechite's lament over the desolation of his fatherland," may be here very appropriately appended. This interesting composition, if not actually written and sung after the carrying away of the statue of the goddess Nanā by the Elamites, might well have been chanted by the sorrowing Erechites on that occasion.

The fragment as published (*Cun. Ins. of W. Asia,* iv. 19, No. 3) begins with the reverse of the text, and breaks off when rather less than half-way through it. Of the obverse, which is as yet unpublished, the remains only of about sixteen lines at the bottom are left. What remains of the obverse refers to the devastation wrought by an enemy in the city of Erech, and the subject is continued on the reverse, which ends in a kind of litany. The following is a free rendering of the inscription on the reverse.

TRANSLATION OF THE LAMENT

How long, my Lady, shall the strong enemy hold thy sanctuary?

There is want in ERECH, thy principal city;

Blood is flowing like water in E-ulbar, the house of thy oracle;

He has kindled and poured out fire like hailstones on all thy lands.

My Lady, sorely am I fettered by misfortune;

My Lady, thou hast surrounded me, and brought me to grief.

The mighty enemy has smitten me down like a single reed.

Not wise myself, I cannot take counsel; ₁

I mourn day and night like the fields. ₂

I, thy servant, pray to thee.

Let thy heart take rest, let thy disposition be softened.

...... weeping, let thy heart take rest.

.... let thy heart take rest.

.... save (?) thou.

Translations of this text have been given by G. Smith, Lenormant, Halévy, Hommel, and Zimmern, and a drawing of the reverse of the fragment, accompanied with a transcription and translation, was given by me in the *Babylonian and Oriental Record* for December 1886.

Footnotes

85:1 Literally, "I do not take counsel, myself I am not wise (Sumerian: *Dimmu nu-mundib, ni-mu nu-mushtugmen;* Assyrian: *Dhême ul tsabtaku, ramani ûl khasaku*).

85:2 Better, perhaps, "Like the *marshland*, day and night I groan."

INSCRIPTION OF TIGLATH-PILESER I, KING OF ASSYRIA— INTRODUCTION

TRANSLATED BY THE EDITOR

THIS inscription of Tiglath-Pileser I. is the longest and most important of the early Assyrian records that have come down to us. The genealogical details given in it are of great value for determining the chronology and succession of the earlier monarchs of Assyria, while the description of the campaigns of the king throws a brilliant and unexpected light on the ancient geography of Western Asia. To the geographer, indeed, the care with which Tiglath-Pileser enumerates the countries he overran and the cities he sacked is of inestimable importance. A new chapter has been added to the history of ancient geography, and we now possess a fairly complete map of the districts north and north-west of Assyria before the overthrow of the Hittite power had brought with it revolution and change. We find geographical names of similar form stretching westwards from the neighbourhood of Lake Van to the confines of Asia Minor, together with evidence that tribes like those of the Moskhi and Tibareni, whose scanty relics in later days found a refuge on the shores of the Black Sea, once inhabited extensive tracts on the slopes of the Taurus Mountains. A new world has, in fact, been opened up to the geographer.

Equally new is the world that has been opened up to the historian. The date of Tiglath-Pileser I can be approximately fixed by the help of an inscription of Sennacherib. On the rock of Bavian (W.A.I. iii. 14, 48-50) Sennacherib refers to "Rimmon and Sala, the gods of the City of Palaces (*Ekallati*), which Merodach-nadin-akhi, King of Accad, had taken and carried away to Babylon in the time of Tiglath-Pileser, King of Assyria"; and he goes on to say that he himself had "brought them out of Babylon 418 years afterwards." As the restoration of the images took place after Sennacherib's destruction of Babylon in B.C. 688, the date of their capture by Merodach-nadin-akhi would be B.C. 1106. The conquests and campaigns described in Tiglath-Pileser's inscription must therefore be placed before this year.

The expeditions of Tiglath-Pileser, however, bore but little fruit. They were not much more than raids, whose effects passed away after the death of the king who conducted them. In a fragmentary inscription of his son and successor, Assur-bil-kala, mention is made of "the land of the west," or Phœnicia, but it is doubtful whether any further campaigns were carried out in this direction. Assyria fell into a state of decay; its frontier cities passed into other hands, and for nearly two hundred years it is hidden altogether from sight. It was not until the ninth century before our era that under the warlike Assur-natsir-pal and his son Shalmaneser II it once more became a name of terror to Western Asia. Tiglath-Pileser I remained the central figure of the older empire, towering above his fellows on the Assyrian throne. When the ancient line of princes became extinct, and the crown was seized by the usurper Pul, the new king knew of no better way in which to legitimise his claim to sovereignty than by assuming the time-honoured name of Tukulti-pal-Esar or Tiglath-Pileser, "the servant of (Uras) the divine son of Esarra."

Though Tiglath-Pileser was not brought into direct relations with Palestine, it is probable that his wars, followed as they were by the temporary decay of Assyria, had much to do with the rise of the empire of David. The wars of Tiglath-Pileser weakened the power of the Hittites in the north, and allowed the small states of Syria to make head against them. For more than a century the latter had no powerful neighbours to fear or court. Egypt had passed under eclipse, and was divided between rival dynasties of kings, while Assyria had equally ceased to be formidable. When David and Joab built up the empire of Israel, there was no strong enemy to oppose and attack them. Hadadezer of Zobah might go "to recover his border at the river" Euphrates; there was no Hittite or Assyrian monarch to stand in his way.

The inscription of Tiglath-Pileser I is inscribed on four large octagonal cylinders of clay, originally buried under the foundations of the four corners of the great temple of Kileh Sherghat, the ancient city of Assur, and now in the British Museum; and it has been published in the *Cuneiform Inscriptions of Western Asia*, i. pl. ix.–xvi. In 1857 the inscription was selected for testing the substantial correctness of the method employed by the Assyriologists, and of the results obtained by them. On the proposal of the Royal Asiatic Society, four translations of it, more or less complete, were made independently by Sir Henry Rawlinson, Mr. Fox Talbot, Dr. Hincks, and Dr. Oppert, and submitted under seal to the secretary of the Society. When opened and compared, it was found that they exhibited a remarkable resemblance to one another as regards both the transliteration of proper names and the rendering of individual passages. The resemblance, in fact, was greater than could be accounted for, except on the assumption that the method employed by the decipherers was a sound one, and that they were working on a solid basis. Since 1857 immense advances have been made in our knowledge of Assyrian. Characters whose values were then unknown, and words whose meaning was obscure, are now familiar to the student; and a historical inscription like that of Tiglath-Pileser presents but few difficulties to the Assyriologist of today.

In 1880 the inscription was re-edited and translated with notes and glossary by Dr. W. Lotz under the auspices of his teacher, Prof. Fr. Delitzsch. The translation embodied all the stores of increased knowledge which the incessant labour of twenty-three years had accumulated, and it is only in a comparatively few passages that it can be improved. The English reader may now consider that he has before him the actual words of the old Assyrian king, and can use them for historical and geographical purposes without fear or reservation. The foot-notes will be found to contain all the geographical information at present attainable relative to the localities mentioned in the text.

A word or two must be added on the name of the divinity to whom Tiglath-Pileser was dedicated by his parents. This deity represented the Sun-god primitively worshipped at Nipur (now Niffer) in Babylonia, who afterwards came to be regarded as a sort of Chaldean Herakles. He is the only deity of the first rank whose name is still a matter of dispute. It is generally given as Adar in default of anything better, but the reading is certainly false. According to the monuments he was called Uras in Accadian, and also in Semitic, when regarded as "the god of light." But he was further known in Assyrian as Baru "the revealer," though we learn from a Babylonian text recently discovered in Upper Egypt that his more usual title was Masu, "the hero," a word which is, letter for letter, the same as the Hebrew Mosheh, "Moses." Masu is defined as being "the Sun-god who rises from the divine day." As such he was identified with one of the primæval gods of Accadian cosmology, and so became " the son of Ê-sarra," or "the house of the firmament." See my *Lectures on the Religion of the Ancient Babylonians*, pp. 151–153.

INSCRIPTION OF TIGLATH-PILESER I—THE BEGINNING! COLUMN I

1. ASUR the great lord, the director of the hosts of the gods,

2. the giver of the sceptre and the crown, the establisher of the kingdom;

3. BEL, the lord (*bilu*), the king of all the spirits of the earth,

4. the father of the gods, the lord of the world;

5. SIN (the Moon-god), the sentient one, the lord of the crown,

6. the exalted one, the god of the storm; 1

7. SAMAS (the Sun-god), the judge of heaven and earth, who beholds

8. the plots of the enemy, who feeds the flock;

9. RIMMON (the Air-god), the prince, the inundator of hostile shores,

10. of countries (and) houses; 2

11. URAS, the hero, the destroyer of evil men and foes,

12. who discloses all that is in the heart;

13. ISHTAR, the eldest of the gods, the lady of girdles,

14. the strengthener of battles.

———————

15. Ye great gods, guiders of heaven (and) earth,

16. whose onset (is) opposition and combat,

17. who have magnified the kingdom

18. of Tiglath-Pileser, the prince, the chosen

19. of the desire of your hearts, the exalted shepherd,

20. whom you have conjured in the steadfastness of your hearts,

21. with a crown supreme you have clothed him; to rule

22. over the land of BEL mightily you have established him;

23. priority of birth, supremacy (and) heroism

24. have you given him; the destiny of his lordship

25. for his increase and supremacy,

26. to inhabit Bit-kharsag-kurkurra 1

27. for ever have you summoned.

———————

28. Tiglath-Pileser, the powerful king,

29. the king of hosts who has no rival, the king of the four zones,

30. the king of all kinglets, the lord of lords, the shepherd-prince, the king of kings,

31. the exalted prophet, 2 to whom by the proclamation of SAMAS

32. the illustrious sceptre has been given as a gift, so that the men

33. who are subject to BEL he has ruled

34. in (their) entirety; the faithful shepherd,

35. proclaimed (lord) over kinglets,

36. the supreme governor whose weapons ASUR

37. has predestined, and for the government of the four zones

38. has proclaimed his name for ever; the capturer

39. of the distant divisions 3 of the frontiers

40. above and below; the illustrious prince

41. whose glory has overwhelmed (all) regions;

42. the mighty destroyer, 1 who like the rush

43. of a flood is made strong against the hostile land;

44. by the proclamation of BEL he has no rival;

45. he has destroyed the foeman of ASUR.

———————

46. May ASUR (and) the great gods who have magnified my kingdom,

47. who have given increase and strength to my fetters,

48. (who) have ordered the boundary of their land

49. to be enlarged, cause my hand to hold

50. their mighty weapons, even the deluge of battle.

51. Countries, mountains,

52. fortresses and kinglets, the enemies of ASSUR,

53. I have conquered, and their territories

54. I have made submit. With sixty kings,

55. I have contended furiously, 2 and

56. power (and) rivalry over them

57. I displayed. A rival in the combat,

58. a confronter in the battle have I not.

59. To the land of ASSYRIA I have added land, to its men

60. (I have added) men; the boundary of my own land

61. I have enlarged, and all their lands I have conquered.

_____

62. At the beginning of my reign twenty thousand men

63. of the MUSKÂYA 3 and their five kings,

64. who for fifty years from the lands of ALZI 4

65. and Purukuzzi had taken the tribute

66. and gifts owing to ASUR my lord,—

67. no king at all in battle

68. had subdued their opposition—to their strength

69. trusted and came down; the land of KUMMUKH 1

70. they seized. Trusting in ASUR my lord

71. I assembled my chariots and armies.

72. Thereupon I delayed not. 2 The mountain of KASI-YARA, 3

73. a difficult region, I crossed,

74. with their twenty thousand fighting men

75. and their five kings in the land of KUMMUKH

76. I contended. A destruction of them

77. I made. The bodies of their warriors

78. in destructive battle like the inundator (RIMMON)

79. I overthrew; their corpses I spread

80. over the valleys and the high places of the mountains.

81. Their heads I cut off; at the sides

82. of their cities I heaped (them) like mounds.

83. Their spoil, their property, their goods,

84. to a countless number I brought forth. Six thousand (men),

85. the relics of their armies, which before

86. my weapons had fled, took

87. my feet. I laid hold upon them and

88. counted them among the men of my own country.

89. In those days, against KUMMUKH, the disobedient,

90. which had withheld the tribute and gifts for ASUR my lord,

91. I marched. The land of KUMMUKH

92. I conquered throughout its circuit.

93. Their spoil, their property, their goods

94. I brought forth; their cities with fire

Footnotes

92:1 Identified with Ea in W.A.I., ii. 60, 21.

92:2 Or "hollows."

93:1 "The Temple of the Mountain of the World," the name of an old temple in the city of Assur, which had been restored by Shalmaneser I (B.C. 1300). In early Babylonian mythology "the Mountain of the World" was the Olympos on which the gods dwelt, and which was identified with Mount Rowandiz. It is referred to in Isaiah xiv. 13, where the Babylonian king is made to say: "I will ascend into heaven, I will exalt my throne above the stars of Elohim: I will sit also on the mount of the assembly (of the gods) in the extremities of the north. I will ascend above the heights of the clouds; I will be like the most High."

93:2 *Isippu*, related to *asipu*, "a diviner," which was borrowed by the Book of Daniel under the form *ashshaph*, and may have the same origin as the name of Joseph.

93:3 *Pulugi*, the Hebrew *Peleg*, in whose days the earth was "divided."

94:1 *Naplu*, probably the same word as the Nephilim or "giants" of Gen. vi. 4 and Numb. xiii. 33. Sennacherib, in describing the construction of his palace, says: "A railing of three bronze cords and the divine Napallu I erected above it," where "the divine Napallu" probably refers to the image of a protecting deity.

94:2 Literally, "in drunken fashion" (*sutkuris*).

94:3 The Meshech of the Old Testament, the Moschi of the classical writers, who in Assyrian times occupied the country to the north of Malatiyeh. In the later Assyrian inscriptions they are associated with the Tubal or Tibareni, as in the Old Testament.

94:4 Alzi lay on the southern bank of the Euphrates, between Palu and Khini, and included Enzite, the Anzitênê of classical geography (at the sources of the Sebbeneh Su). Alzi was invaded by the Vannic king Menuas, who says that it formed part of the territory of the Khate or Hittites.

95:1 Kummukh, the classical Komagêne, extended in the Assyrian age on either side of the Euphrates, from Malatiyeh in the north to Birejik in the south, Merash probably being one of its cities.

95:2 Literally, "I awaited not the future."

95:3 Mons Masius, the modern Tur Abdin.

COLUMN II

1. I burned, I threw down, I dug up. The rest

2. of (the men of) KUMMUKH, who before my weapons

3. had fled, to the city of SERESSE ₁

4. on the further bank of the TIGRIS

5. passed over; the city for their stronghold

6. they made. My chariots and warriors

7. I took. The difficult mountains and their inaccessible

8. paths with picks of bronze

9. I split. A pontoon for the passage

10. of my chariots and army I contrived.

11. The TIGRIS I crossed. The city of SERISE,

12. their strong city, I captured.

13. Their fighting men, in the midst of the mountains,

14. I flung to the ground like sling-stones (?). 2

15. Their corpses over the TIGRIS and the high places of the mountains

16. I spread. In those days the armies

17. of the land of QURKHÊ, 3 which for the preservation

18. and help of the land of KUMMUKH

19. had come, along with the armies

20. of KUMMUKH, like a moon-stone I laid low.

21. The corpses of their fighting men into heaps

22. in the ravines of the mountains I heaped up;

23. the bodies of their soldiers the river NAME

24. carried away into the TIGRIS.

25. Kili-anteru the son of Kali-anteru,

26. (the descendant) of 'Saru-pin-'siusuni, 1

27. their king in the midst of battle my hand

28. captured; his wives (and) children

29. the offspring of his heart, his troops, 180

30. bronze plates, 5 bowls of copper,

31. along with their gods, gold (and) silver,

32. the choicest of their property, I removed.

33. Their spoil (and) their goods I carried away.

34. The city itself and its palace with fire

35. I burned, I pulled down, (and) dug up.

---

36. As for the city of URRAKHINAS, their stronghold,

37. which was situated on the mountain of PANARI,

38. fear that avoided the glory of ASSUR my lord

39. overwhelmed them. To save

40. their lives they removed their gods;

41. to the ravines of the lofty mountains

42. they fled like a bird. My chariots

43. and armies I took; I crossed the TIGRIS.

44. Sadi-anteru, the son of Khattukhi, 2 the king

45. of URRAKHINAS, that he might not be conquered,

46. in that country took my feet.

47. The children, the offspring of his heart, and his family

48. I took as hostages.

49. Sixty bronze plates, a bowl of copper,

50. and a tray of heavy copper,

51. along with 120 men, oxen,

52. (and) sheep, as tribute and offering

53. (which) he brought, I received. I had compassion on him;

54. I granted his life. The heavy yoke

55. of my lordship I laid upon him for future days.

56. The broad land of KUMMUKH throughout its circuit

57. I conquered; under my feet I subdued.

58. In those days a tray of copper (and) a bowl

59. of copper, from the spoil and tribute

60. of KUMMUKH I dedicated to ASUR my lord.

61. The sixty bronze plates along with their gods

62. I presented to RIMMON who loves me.

———————

63. Through the violence of my powerful weapons, which ASSUR the lord

64. gave for strength and heroism,

65. in thirty of my chariots that go at my side

66. my fleet steeds 1 (and) my soldiers,

67. who are strong 2 in destructive fight,

68. I took; against the country of MILDIS, the powerful,

69. the disobedient, I marched. Mighty mountains,

70. an inaccessible district,

71. (where it was) good in my chariots (where it was) bad on my feet,

72. I crossed. At the mountain of ARUMA,

73. a difficult district, which for the passage of my chariots

74. was not suited, I left the chariots,

75. I took the lead of my soldiers.

76. Like a lion (?) the obstacles (?) in the ravines of the inaccessible mountains

77. victoriously I crossed.

78. The land of MILDIS like the flood ₃ of the deluge I overwhelmed.

79. Their fighting men in the midst of battle

80. like a moon-stone I laid low. Their spoil

81. their goods (and) their property I carried away.

82. All their cities I burned with fire.

83. Hostages, tribute and offering

84. I imposed upon them.

---

85. Tiglath-pileser, the hero, the warrior,

86. who opens the path of the mountains,

87. who subdues the disobedient, who sweeps away

88. all the overweening.

---

89. The land of SUBARI, ₁ the powerful, the disobedient,

90. I subdued. As for the countries of ALZI

91. and PURUKUZZI, which had withheld

92. their tribute and their offering,

93. the heavy yoke of my lordship upon them

94. I laid; (saying), each year tribute and offering

95. to my city of ASUR, to my presence,

96. let them bring. In accordance with my valour,

97. since ASUR the lord has caused my hand to hold

98. the mighty weapon which subdues the disobedient, and

99. to enlarge the frontier of his country

100. has commanded (me), 4000 men of the KASKÂ 2

101. and of the URUMÂ, 3 soldiers of the HITTITES (KHATTÎ),

102. disobedient ones, who in their strength

Footnotes

96:1 This must have been in the neighbourhood of Amid or Diarbekir. The Vannic king Menuas mentions a Hittite city, Surisidas, in the vicinity of Alzi. Delitzsch compares the Sareisa of Strabo.

96:2 *Sutmasi*. In R. 204. i. 22 *sa sammasi* is interpreted "a slinger," and in W.A.I., iv. 13, 5, *samsû* is "a sling-stone."

96:3 The land of Qurkhi extended eastward of Diarbekir, along the northern bank of the Tigris. The name is preserved in that of Kurkh, 20 miles S. E. of Diarbekir, where there are ruins, and where a stêlê of Shalmaneser II has been discovered.

97:1 Sarpina was the name of one of the Hittite cities, whose god was invoked in the treaty between Ramses II and the Hittite king. With the termination we may compare that of Abar-'siuni in iv. 82.

97:2 The first part of the name Sadi-anteru, which reminds us of the Lydian Sady-attês, may contain the name of the god Sanda or Sandon. A Hittite prince mentioned by the Vannic king Menuas was called Sada-hadas. Khattu-khi means "the Hittite," the suffix - *khi*, as in Vannic, denoting a patronymic or gentilic adjective. Urra-khi-nas is similarly derived from Urra, the termination - *khi-nas*, in Vannic, denoting "the place of the people of."

98:1 Literally " complete horses."

98:2 *Liê*.

98:3 Literally "mound" or "tel."

99:1 Subari, called Subarti a few lines farther on, had been overrun by Rimmon-nirari I. (B.C. 1330), and was afterwards conquered by Assur-natsir-pal, who describes it as situated between Qurkhi and Nirib, or the plain of Diarbekir. As Qurkhi lay "opposite the land of the Hittites," Subari would have adjoined the territory of the latter people, in the immediate vicinity of Alzi and Purukuzzi.

99:2 This seems to be the same word as the Kolkhians of classical geography, though the seat of the Kolkhians was far to the north of that of the Kaskâ. In the classical period, however, we find that the Moschi and Tibareni (Meshech and Tubal) had also shifted far to the north of their habitat in Assyrian times, and like the Kolkhians had settled on the shores of the Black Sea. A town of Kolkhis, now represented by the name of Lake Goldshik, lay to the S. W. of Palu.

99:3 Uruma may be the Urima of classical geography, the modern Urum. It is called Urume of Bitanu by Assur-natsir-pal, Bitanu being the district south of Lake Van.

COLUMN III

1. had seized the cities of SUBARTI which looked to

2. the face ₁ of ASUR my lord,

3. heard of my march against the land of SUBARTI;

4. the glory of my valour overwhelmed them;

5. they avoided battle; my feet

6. they took.

7. Together with their property and 120

8. chariots (and the horses) harnessed to their yokes

9. I took them; as the men

10. of my own country I counted them.

---

11. In the fierceness of my valour for the second time

12. to the country of KUMMUKH I marched. All

13. their cities I captured. Their spoil

14. their goods and their property I carried away.

15. Their cities with fire I burned,

16. I threw down (and) dug up, and the relics

17. of their armies, who before my powerful weapons

18. were terror-stricken and the onset of my mighty battle

19. avoided, to save

20. their lives sought the mighty summits

21. of the mountains, an inaccessible region.

22. To the fastnesses of the lofty ranges

23. and the ravines of the inaccessible mountains

24. which were unsuited for the tread of men

25. I ascended after them. Trial of weapons, combat

26. and battle they essayed with me.

27. A destruction of them I made. The bodies

28. of their warriors in the ravines of the mountains

29. like the inundator (RIMMON) I overthrew. Their corpses

30. over the valleys and high places of the mountains

31. I spread. Their spoil, their goods

32. and their property from the mighty

33. summits of the mountains I brought down.

34. The land of KUMMUKH to its whole extent I subjugated, and

35. added to the territory of my country.

_____

36. Tiglath-pileser the powerful king,

37. the mighty overwhelmer of the disobedient, he who sweeps away

38. the opposition of the wicked.

_____

39. In the supreme power of ASUR my lord

40. against the land of KHARIA 1 and the widespread armies

41. of the land of QURKHI,—lofty mountain-ranges

42. whose site no king at all

43. had sought out—ASUR the lord commanded (me)

44. to march. My chariots and armies

45. I assembled. The neighbourhood 2 of the mountains of IDNI

46. and AYA, an inaccessible district, I reached,

47. lofty mountains, which like the point of a sword

48. were formed, which for the passage of my chariots

49. were unsuited. The chariots in idleness

50. I left there. The precipitous mountains

51. I crossed. All the land of QURKHI

52. had collected its widespread armies, and

53. to make trial of arms, combat and battle

54. in the mountain of AZUTABGIS 3 was stationed, and

55. in the mountain, an inaccessible spot, with them

56. I fought, a destruction of them I made.

57. The bodies of their warriors on the high places of the mountains

58. into heaps I heaped.

59. The corpses of their warriors over the valleys and high places

60. of the mountains I spread. Against the cities

61. which were situated in the ravines of the mountains fiercely

62. I pierced (my way). ꜝ Twenty-five cities of the land of KHARIA

63. which lie at the foot of the mountains of AYA, SUIRA, IDNI,

64. SIZU, SELGU, ARZANIBIU, URU'SU, and ANITKU,

65. I captured. Their spoil,

66. their goods and their property I carried off.

67. Their cities with fire I burned,

68. I threw down (and) dug up.

---

69. The country of ADAUS feared the onset of my mighty battle,

70. and their dwelling-place (the inhabitants) abandoned.

71. To the ravines of the lofty mountains

72. like birds they fled. The glory of ASSUR my lord

73. overwhelmed them, and

74. they descended and took my feet.

75. Tribute and offering I imposed upon them.

76. The lands of 'SARAUS and AMMAUS

77. which from days immemorial had not known

78. subjection, like the flood of the deluge

79. I overwhelmed. With their armies

80. on the mountain of ARUMA 2 I fought, and

81. a destruction of them I made. The bodies

82. of their fighting-men like sling-stones (?)

83. I flung to the ground. Their cities I captured.

84. Their gods I removed. Their spoil,

85. their goods (and) their property I carried away.

86. Their cities with fire I burned,

87. I threw down (and) dug up; to mounds and ruins

88. I reduced. The heavy yoke of my lordship

89. I laid upon them. The face of ASSUR my lord

90. I made them behold. 1

91. The powerful countries of I'SUA 2 and DARIA

92. which were disobedient I conquered. Tribute

93. and offering I imposed upon them.

94. The face of ASSUR my lord I caused them to behold.

95. In my supremacy when my enemies

96. I had conquered, my chariots and armies

97. I took. The lower Zab 3

98. I crossed. The countries of MURATTAS and SARADAUS

99. which are in the midst of the mountains of A'SANIU andADHUMA

100. an inaccessible region, I conquered.

101. Their armies like lambs

102. I cut down. The city of MURATTAS,

103. their stronghold, in the third part of a day

104. from sunrise I captured.

105. Their gods, their goods, (and) their property,

106. 60 plates of bronze,

Footnotes

100:1 That is, were subject to.

101:1 It is clear that Kharia was a district of Qurkhi which lay eastward of Diarbekir and the Supnat or Sebeneh Su, in the direction of Bitlis. It is perhaps the Arua of Assur-natsir-pal which adjoined the western frontier of Ararat, a kingdom at that time confined to Lake Van and the district south of the Lake. The name reminds us of the classical Korra, now Karia, a little to the south-east of Kolkhis (on Lake Goldshik), and to the north-west of Diarbekir.

101:2 *Birti*, from *baru* "to see."

101:3 Perhaps to be read Azues.

102:1 *Aznig*, not *a'snig*.

102:2 As, according to ii. 78, Aruma lay on the frontier of Mildis, Adaus, 'Saraus, and Ammaus must have been Kurdish districts to the eastward of Kummukh. The country of Adaus is mentioned by Assur-natsir-pal in connection with Kirruri, which lay between Nimme and Qurkhi.

103:1 That is, "I reduced them to subjection to Assur."

103:2 I'sua, according to Shalmaneser II, adjoined Enzite or Anzitênê (on the Sebbeneh Su) and lay on the southern bank of the Arsanias between Palu and Mush. It is probably the U'su of Assur-natsir-pal, on the western frontier of Arua (see note on iii. 40).

103:3 The lower Zab falls into the Tigris a little below Kalah Sherghat (Assur). It rises in the Kurdish mountains, flowing past Arbela, and was called Kapros by the classical geographers in contradistinction to the Lykos or Upper Zab.

COLUMN IV

1. 30 talents of bronze in fragments, ₄ (and) the smaller furniture

2. of their palace, their spoil

3. I carried away. The city itself with fire

4. I burned, I threw down (and) dug up.

5. In those days that bronze

6. I dedicated to RIMMON the great lord who loves me.

----

7. In the mightiness of the power of ASUR my lord

8. against the lands of 'SUGI and QURKHI, which had not submitted

9. to ASUR my lord, I marched. With 6000

10. of their troops from the lands of KHIME, LUKHI,

11. ARIRGI, ALAMUN,

12. NIMNI and all the land of QURKHI

13. far-extending, on the mountain of KHIRIKHI,

14. an inaccessible district, which like the point of a sword

15. was formed, with all those countries

16. on my feet I fought.

17. A destruction of them I made.

18. Their fighting-men in the ravines of the mountains

19. into heaps I heaped.

20. With the blood of their warriors the mountain of KHIRIKHI

21. like *wool* (?) I dyed.

22. The land of 'SUGI throughout its circuit I conquered

23. Their 25 gods, their spoil,

24. their goods (and) their property I carried away.

25. All their cities with fire

26. I burnt, I threw down (and) dug up.

27. Those who were left of their armies took my feet;

28. I showed favour towards them.

29. Tribute and offering upon them

30. I imposed; along with those who behold the face

31. of ASUR my lord I counted them.

32. In those days the 25 gods of those lands,

———————

33. the acquisitions of my hands,

34. which I had taken, to gratify (?) the temple of BELTIS

35. the great wife, the favourite of ASUR my lord,

36. ANU, RIMMON (and) ISHTAR Of ASSUR,

37. as well as the palaces of my city ASSUR

38. and the goddesses of my country

39. I gave.

---

40. Tiglath-pileser the powerful king,

41. the conqueror of hostile regions, the rival

42. of the company of all kings.

---

43. In those days through the supreme power

44. of ASUR my lord, through the everlasting grace

45. of SAMAS the warrior, through the ministry

46. of the great gods, who in the four zones

47. rule in righteousness, and have no vanquisher

48. in the combat, no rival in the battle,

49. to the lands of distant kings

50. on the shore of the upper sea, ı

51. who knew not subjection,

52. ASUR the lord urged me and I went.

53. Difficult paths and trackless passes

54. whose interior in former days

55. no king at all had known,

56. steep roads, ways

57. unopened, I traversed.

58. The mountains of ELAMA, AMADANA, 2 ELKHIS,

59. SIRABELI, TARKHUNA,

60. TIRKA-KHULI, KIZRA,

61. TARKHA-NABE, 3 ELULA,

62. KHASTARAE, SAKHISARA,

63. UBERA, MILI-ADRUNI,

64. SULIANZI, NUBANÂSI,

65. and SESI, 16 mighty mountains,

66. where the ground was good in my chariots, where it was difficult

67. with picks of bronze, I penetrated.

68. I cut down the *urum* -trees which grow in the mountains.

69. Bridges for the passage

70. of my troops I constructed well.

71. I crossed the EUPHRATES. The king of the land of Nimme, 1

72. the king of TUNUBU, 2 the king of TUALI,

73. the king of QIDARI, the king of UZULA,

74. the king of UNZAMUNI, the king of ANDIABE,

75. the king of PILAQINI, the king of ADHURGINI,

76. the king of KULI-BARZINI, 3 the king of SINIBIRNI,

77. the king of KHIMUA, the king of PAITERI, 4

78. the king of UIRAM, the king of SURURIA,

79. the king of ABAENI, 5 the king of ADAENI,

80. the king of KIRINI, the king of ALBAYA,

81. the king of UGINA, the king of NAZABIA,

82. the king of ABAR-'SIUNI, (and) the king of DAYAENI, 6

83. all the 23 kings of the countries of NAIRI, 7

84. in the midst of their lands assembled

85. their chariots and their armies, and

86. to make conflict and battle

87. came on. With the violence of my powerful

88. weapons I pierced them.

89. An overthrow of their widespread armies

90. like the inundation of RIMMON

91. I made. The bodies of their warriors

92. in the plains, the high places of the mountain, and the walls

93. of their cities like *sling-stones* (?)

94. I flung to the ground. One hundred and twenty of their yoke-chariots

95. in the midst of the combat

96. I acquired. Sixty kings

97. of the lands of NAIRI in addition to those who

98. had gone to their assistance

99. with my mace I pursued

100. as far as the Upper Sea.

101. Their great fortresses I captured.

Footnotes

103:4 This seems to be the meaning of *sabartum* in K 1999, i. 15.

105:1 That is, Lake Van.

105:2 Amadana was the district about Amida or Diarbekir. Assur-natsir-pal reached Amadana after leaving Adana, a district of Qurkhi.

105:3 Compare the names of the Gamgumian and Melitenian princes Tarkhu-lara and Tarkhu-nazi, and of the Hittite city Tarkhi-gamas mentioned by the Vannic king Menuas.

106:1 Nimme, according to Assur-natsir-pal, adjoined Alzi and Dayaeni in the neighbourhood of Mush.

106:2 This must be the Dhunibun of Shalmaneser II, eastward of the sources of the Tigris, on the river of Mush (the modern Kara Su).

106:3 In the Vannic language the termination *ni* (*s*) denoted "belonging to," and *barzini* or *barzani* signified "a chapel."

106:4 The Vannic king calls the district in which Palu stands "the land of Puterias."

106:5 Perhaps the Abunis of the Vannic inscriptions.

106:6 Dayaeni was on the northern bank of the Arsanias, to the north of Mush. It is called the kingdom of "the son of Diaus" in the Vannic texts, which define it more closely as situated on the Murad Chai, near Melazgherd.

106:7 The land of Nairi or "the rivers" denoted in the age of Tiglath-Pileser I. the districts at the sources of the Tigris and the Euphrates. In the time of Assur-natsir-pal and his successors, on the other hand, it was the country between Lake Van and the northern frontier of Assyria, and consequently lay to the south-west of the Nairi of the time of Tiglath-Pileser I. It will be noticed that there was as yet no kingdom of Ararat or Van.

COLUMN V

1. Their spoil, their goods (and) their property

2. I carried away. Their cities with fire

3. I burned, I threw down (and) dug up,

4. I reduced to mounds and ruins.

5. Large troops of horses,

6. mules, calves, and the possessions

7. of their homesteads to a countless number

8. I brought back. All the kings

9. of the countries of NAIRI alive my hand

10. captured. To those kings

11. I extended mercy, and

12. spared their lives. Their captivity

13. and their bondage in the presence of SAMAS my lord

14. I liberated, and an oath by my great

15. gods ı unto future days for ever

16. and ever that they should be (my) servants I made them swear.

17. The children, the offspring of their kingdom,

18. as hostages I took.

19. Twelve hundred horses (and) 2000 oxen

20. I imposed upon them as tribute.

21. In their countries I left them.

---

22. 'Siena king of DAYAENI,

23. who did not submit to ASUR my lord,

24. captive and bound to my city

25. of ASUR I brought; mercy

26. I extended to him, and from my city of ASUR,

27. as the exalter of the great gods

28. unto exaltation, alive

29. I let him depart. The lands of NAIRI,

30. far-extending, I subdued throughout their whole extent,

31. and all their kings

32. I reduced beneath my feet.

---

33. In the course of the same campaign

34. against the city of MILIDIA, 1 of the country of KHANI 2 the great,

35. violent (and) unsubmissive, I marched.

36. The mighty onset of my battle they feared.

37. My feet they took; I had mercy on them.

38. The city itself I did not capture; their hostages

39. I accepted. A homer by way of tax of lead

40. as an annual tribute

41. not to be intermitted I imposed upon them.

42. Tiglath-pileser, the destroyer, the quick-moving,

43. the implacable, the deluge of battle.

———————

44. In the service of ASUR my lord, my chariots

45. and warriors I took. In the desert

46. I made (my way). To the bank of the waters

47. of the land of the ARMAYANS, 1 the enemies of ASUR my lord,

48. I marched. From opposite to the land of 'SUKHI, 2

49. as far as the city of GARGAMIS, 3 of the land of the HITTITES (*Khatti*),

50. in one day I plundered.

51. Their soldiers I slew. Their spoil,

52. their goods and their possessions

53. to a countless number I carried back.

54. The remains of their armies,

55. who before the powerful (weapons) of ASUR my lord

56. had fled and had crossed the EUPHRATES,

57. after them in vessels of *inflated* (?) skins 4

58. I crossed the EUPHRATES;

59. six of their cities which (were) at the foot of Mount BISRI 5

60. I captured; with fire I burned,

61. I threw down (and) dug up. Their spoil, their goods

62. and their possessions to my city of ASUR

63. I brought.

---

64. Tiglath-pileser, the trampler upon the mighty,

65. the slaughterer of the unsubmissive, who weakens 6

66. utterly the strong.

---

67. To conquer the land of MU'SRI 7 ASUR the lord

68. urged me, and between the mountains of ELAMUNI

69. TALA and KHARU'SA I made (my way).

70. I conquered the land of MU'SRI throughout its circuit,

71. I massacred their warriors.

72. The cities I burned with fire, I threw down,

73. I dug up. The armies of the land of QUMANÎ

74. to the help of the land of MU'SRI

75. had gone. On a mountain with them

76. I fought. A destruction of them I made.

77. To a single city, ARINI, at the foot of mount AI'SA,

78. I drove and shut them up. My feet

79. they took. The city itself I spared.

80. Hostages, tribute and offering

81. I laid upon them.

82. In those days all the land of QUMANÎ,

83. which had prepared to help MU'SRI,

84. gathered together all those countries, and

85. to make conflict and battle

86. were determined. With the violence of my powerful weapons,

87. with 20,000 of their numerous troops

88. on mount TALA I fought.

89. A destruction of them I made.

90. Their strong forces I broke through.

91. As far as mount KHARU'SA, which (is) in front of the land of MU'SRI,

92. I pursued their fugitives. The bodies

93. of their warriors in the ravines of the mountain

94. like a moon-stone I flung to the ground.

95. Their corpses over the valleys and the high places of the mountains

96. I spread. Their great fortresses

97. I captured, with fire I burned,

98. I threw down (and) dug up, so that they became mounds and ruins.

99. KHUNU'SA their fortified city

100. like the flood of the deluge I overwhelmed.

Footnotes

107:1 Literally "the bann (*mamit*) of my great gods."

108:1 The classical Melitênê, now Malatiyeh, on the Euphrates.

108:2 This district of Kappadokia is called "Khani the Great," to distinguish it from another Khani near Babylon, whose king Tukulti-mer, son of Ilu-saba, dedicated a bronze ram's head, now in the British Museum, to the temple of the Sun-god at Sippara.

109:1 The Arameans.

109:2 The Shuhites of the Old Testament, who extended along the western banks of the Euphrates from the mouth of the Khabour to above that of the Belikh. "Bildad the Shuhite" (Job ii. II) would be Bel-Dadda, Dadda, as we learn from the cuneiform inscriptions, being a form of Hadad, the Syrian name of the god of heaven.

109:3 Carchemish, the Hittite capital on the Euphrates, between the mouth of the Sajur and Birejik, now represented by the mounds of Jerablûs.

109:4 *Sugase*, borrowed from the Accadian *'su*, "skin," and *gavsia* (whence the Semitic *gubsu*).

109:5 Now Tel-Basher.

109:6 *Musarbibu*, "subduer," according to M. Amiaud, who regards the word as an example of a *parel* conjugation (*Revue d'Assyriologie*, ii. 1, p. 12).

109:7 Mu'sri or Muzri lay to the north-east of Khorsabad, in the mountainous district now inhabited by the Missouri Kurds. The tribute of a rhinoceros, yak, elephant, and apes, brought by its inhabitants to Shalmaneser II, must be explained on the supposition that the caravan road from the east passed through it.

COLUMN VI

1. With their mighty armies

2. in the city and the mountains I contended furiously.

3. A destruction of them I made.

4. Their fighting men in the midst of the mountains

5. like a moon-stone I flung down. Their heads

6. like (that) of a sheep I cut off.

7. Their corpses over the valleys and high places of the mountains

8. I spread. The city itself I captured.

9. Their gods I carried away. Their goods (and) their property

10. I brought out. The city with fire I burned.

11. Three of their great fortresses, which of brickwork

12. were constructed, and the circuit of the city itself

13. I threw down (and) dug up; to mounds and ruins

14. I reduced (them), and *salt* (?) on the top of them

15. I sowed. A plate of bronze I made;

16. the conquest of the lands, which through ASUR my god (and) my lord

17. I had conquered, that the site of this city should not (again) be taken,

18. nor its wall be constructed, upon (it)

19. I wrote. A house of brick on the top of it

20. I built: these plates of bronze

21. in the midst (of it) I placed.

_____

22. In the service of ASUR my lord my chariots

23. and soldiers I took. The city of KIPSUNA

24. their royal city I besieged. The QUMANIANS

25. feared the mighty, onset of my battle;

26. my feet they took; their lives I spared.

27. Its great wall and its gate-posts

28. of bricks I ordered to be destroyed, and

29. from their foundations to their coping

30. they were thrown down and turned into a mound;

3r. and 300 families of evil-doers

32. who (were) within it, who were not submissive to ASUR my lord,

33. were removed (out of it). I received them. Their hostages

34. I took. Tribute and offering

35. above what was previously paid upon them

36. I imposed, and the widespread land of QUMANÎ

37. throughout its circuit under my feet

38. I subdued.

---

39. In all, 42 countries and their kings

40. from the fords of the lower ZAB

41. (and) the border of the distant mountains

42. to the fords of the EUPHRATES,

43. the land of the HITTITES (*Khattê*) and the Upper Sea

44. of the setting sun, ₁ from the beginning of my sovereignty

45. until my fifth year my hand has conquered.

46. One word in unison have I made them utter.

47. Their hostages have I taken. Tribute

48. and offering have I imposed upon them.

---

49. I left the numerous roads of foreign peoples

50. which were not attached to my empire:

51. where the ground was favourable in my chariots, and where it was difficult

52. on my feet, after them

53. I marched. The feet of the enemy

54. I kept from my land.

---

55. Tiglath-pileser the valiant hero,

56. the holder of the sceptre unrivalled

57. who completes the mission of the supreme (gods).

58. URAS and NERGAL have given their forceful

59. weapons and their supreme bow

60. to the hands of my lordship.

61. Under the protection of URAS who loves me

62. from young wild bulls, powerful (and) large,

63. in the desert in the land of MITÂNI

64. and in the city of ARAZIGI, ι which (is) in front

65. of the land of the HITTITES, with my mighty bow,

66. a lasso of iron and my pointed

67. spear, their lives I ended:

68. their hides (and) their horns

69. to my city of ASUR I brought.

———————

70. Ten powerful male-elephants ₂

71. in the land of HARRAN (*Kharrani*) and (on) the bank of the KHABUR

72. I slew. Four elephants alive

73. I captured. Their hides

74. (and) their teeth along with the live

75. elephants I brought to my city ASUR.

———————

76. Under the protection of URAS who loves me

77. 120 lions, with my stout heart,

78. in the conflict of my heroism

79. on my feet I slew;

80. and 800 lions in my chariot

81. with javelins (?) I slaughtered.

82. All the cattle of the field and the birds of heaven

83. that fly, among my rarities ₃

84. I placed.

———————

85. After that the enemies of ASUR throughout their territories

86. I had conquered, the temple of ISTAR of (the city) ASSUR

87. my lady, the temple of RIMMON, 1 (and) the temple of the OLDER BEL, 2

88. the temple of the Divinities, 3 the temples of the gods

89. of my city ASUR, which were decayed, I built,

90. I completed. The entrances of their temples

91. I constructed. The great gods, my lords,

92. I introduced within;

93. I rejoiced the heart of their great divinity.

94. The palaces, the seat of sovereignty

95. belonging to the great fortresses

96. on the borders of my country, which from

97. the time of my fathers through long

98. years had been deserted and ruined and

99. were destroyed, I built (and) completed.

100. The castles of my country that were overthrown

101. I enclosed. The conduits 4 throughout all the land of ASSYRIA

102. I fastened together wholly, and an accumulation

103. of grain in addition to that (collected) by my fathers

104. I brought back (and) heaped up.

105. Troops of horses, oxen (and) asses

Footnotes

112:1 That is, Lake Van.

113:1 Arazig is the Eragiza of Ptolemy, on the Euphrates, to the north of Balis and the south of Carchemish. Mitâni seems to be the Matenau of the Egyptians mentioned by Ramses III immediately before Carchemish.

113:2 I follow Lotz in this rendering.

113:3 *Ni'siggi*, borrowed from the Sumerian *nin-'sig*, "secret."

114:1 Here called Mâtu, "the god of the tempest."

114:2 Bel of Nipur, called Mul-lil, "the lord of the ghost-world," by the Accadians, and distinguished from Bel Merodach, the younger Bel of Babylon.

114:3 This apparently means that the images of several deities were collected together in the temple of the Older Bel.

114:4 Literally "sewers."

COLUMN VII

1. which in the service of ASUR my lord

2. in the countries which I had conquered,

3. as the acquisition of my hands

4. which I took, I collected together, and troops.

5. of goats, fallow-deer, wild sheep,

6. (and) antelopes which ASUR and URAS

7. the gods who love me have given

8. for hunting, in the midst of the lofty

9. mountains I have taken;

10. their herds I enclosed,

11. their number like that of a flock

12. of sheep I counted:

13. young lambs, the offspring

14. of their heart, according to the desire of my heart,

15. along with my pure sacrifices

16. annually I sacrificed to ASUR my lord.

———————

17. The cedar, the *likkarin* tree

18. (and) the *allakan* tree from the countries

19. which I had conquered, these trees

20. which among the kings

21. my fathers who (were) before (me) none

22. had planted, I took and

23. in the plantations of my country

24. I planted, and the costly fruit

25. of the plantation, which did not exist in my country,

26. I took. The plantations of ASSYRIA

27. I established.

———————

28. Chariots (and horses) bound to the yoke,

29. for the mightiness of my country, more than before

30. I introduced (and) harnessed.

31. To the land of ASUR (I added) land,

32. to its people I added people.

33. The health of my people I improved.

34. A peaceable habitation

35. I caused them to inhabit.

---

36. Tiglath-pileser, the great, the supreme,

37. whom ASUR and URAS according to the desire

38. of his heart conduct, so that

39. after the enemies of ASUR

40. he has overrun all their territories, and

41. has utterly slaughtered the overweening.

42. The son of Asur-ris-ilim, ₁ the powerful king, the conqueror

43. of hostile lands, the subjugator

44. of all the mighty.

---

45. The grandson of Mutaggil-Nu'sku, whom ASUR the great lord

46. in the conjuration of his steadfast heart

47. had required, and to the shepherding

48. of the land of Asur had raised securely.

---

49. The true son of Asur-da'an,

50. the upraiser of the illustrious sceptre, who ruled

51. the people of BEL, ₂ who the work of his hands

52. and the gift of his sacrifice

53. commended to the great gods, so that

54. he arrived at gray hairs and old age.

---

55. The descendant of Uras-pileser,

56. the guardian (?) king, the favourite of ASUR,

57. whose might ₃ like a sling

58. was spread over his country, and

59. the armies of ASUR he shepherded faithfully.

---

60. In those days the temple of ANU and RIMMON

61. the great gods, my lords,

62. which in former times Samas-Rimmon, the high-priest ₁ of ASUR,

63. the son of Isme-Dagon, the high-priest also of ASUR,

64. built, for 641 years

65. went on decaying,—

66. Asur-da'an the king of ASUR,

67. the son of Uras-pileser, the king also of ASUR,

68. pulled down this temple (but) did not rebuild (it);

69. for 60 years its foundations

70. were not laid.

---

71. At the beginning of my reign, ANU

72. and RIMMON the great gods, my lords,

73. who love my priesthood (*'sanguti*),

74. commanded the rebuilding

75. of their habitation. I made bricks;

76. I purified its site;

77. I undertook its reconstruction; 2 its foundations

78. I laid upon the mass of a huge mound.

79. This place throughout its circuit

80. I piled up with bricks like a double fold (?).

81. Fifty *tibki* 3 below

82. I sunk (it); upon it

83. the foundations of the temple of ANU and RIMMON

84. I laid with *pulu* -stone. 4

85. From its foundations to its roof

86. I built (the temple); greater than (it was) before I reared (it).

87. Two great towers

88. which for the glorification of their great divinities

89. were adapted, I constructed.

90. The illustrious temple, a building with cornices, 1

91. the seat of their rejoicing,

92. the habitation of their pleasure,

93. which has been beautified like the star(s) of heaven,

94. and by the art of the workmen

95. has been richly carved,

96. I have worked at, have toiled over, have built

97. (and) have completed. Its interior

98. I compacted together like the heart of heaven;

99. its walls like the resplendence

100. of the rising of the stars I adorned.

101. I strengthened its buttresses,

102. and its towers to heaven

103. I lifted; and its roof

104. I fastened together with brickwork.

105. The divining rod, 2

106. the oracle of their great

107. divinities within it

108. I placed.

109. ANU and RIMMON, the great gods

110. I introduced within (it);

111. on their thrones supreme

112. I seated them;

113. and the heart of their great divinities

114. I gladdened.

Footnotes

116:1 Sir H. Rawlinson has suggested that Asur-ris-ilim is the Chushan-rish-athaim of Judges iii. 8, a name which certainly seems to be corrupt. Chushan-rish-athaim is called king of Aram Naharaim or "Aram of the two rivers," which represents Mesopotamia in the Old Testament, though the Naharaina of the Egyptian monuments was the region about the Orontes, while the Assyrian Nahri or Nairi was primarily the district to the northwest of Lake Van, and afterwards the country to the south of it. Assur-ris-ilim claims to have "subdued Lullumi and all Quti (or Kurdistan) with the entrance to its mountain-ranges" (W.A.I., iii. 3, 18); but these districts lay to the east of Assyria, and no allusion is made to any campaign in the west.

116:2 That is, the Babylonians.

116:3 Literally "fulness" (*nubalu*, akin to *nabli*, in the Cuthean Legend of the Creation, iv. 20).

117:1 *Pate'si.*

117:2 Literally "I took its strength" (read *dannat-su*, not *libnat-su*).

117:3 The *tibku* was a measure of length which is explained in the Talmud as the longer cubit of 7 palms mentioned in 2 Chr. iii. 3.

117:4 Prof. D. H. Müller believes the *pulu* -stone to have been brought from Armenia, and to have derived its name from the Vannic *pulu-'si*, "engraved." It is also called *pili* -stone. It was a species of white marble.

118:1 *Qusuda.* In W.A.I., V. 28, 4, *gasdu* is the synonym of *allum*, the Aramaic *êlâ*.

118:2 *Elallâ.* It seems to have been a stem of papyrus covered with writing.

COLUMN VIII

1. BIT-KHAMRI (the temple) of RIMMON,

2. which Samas-Rimmon the high-priest of ASSUR 3

3. the son of Isme-Dagon the high-priest of ASUR

4. had built, had fallen into decay and was ruined.

5. I purified its site; from its foundations

6. to its roof with brick

7. I bonded (it) together. More than before

8. I adorned, I established (it).

9. In its midst pure victims

10. to RIMMON my lord I sacrificed.

———————

11. In those days the *ivory* (?) stone, the *khalta* stone

12. and the mountain stone from the mountains

13. of NAIRI, 1 which through ASUR my lord

14. I had conquered, I carried away;

15. in BIT-KHAMRI, (the temple) of RIMMON my lord

16. for days to come I set (them).

———————

17. As I the illustrious temple, the building supreme,

18. for the habitation of ANU and RIMMON the great gods

19. my lords, have laboured at and have not desisted

20. (and) have not rested from the work, 2

21. (but) have quickly completed (it), and

22. have gladdened the heart of their great

23. divinity, (so) may ANU and RIMMON

24. turn (to me) for ever and

25. love the lifting up of my hands;

26. may they hearken to the earnestness of my prayer;

27. abundant rains, years

28. of fertility and fatness to my reign

29. may they give; in battle and conflict

30. may they conduct (me) in safety;

31. all the countries of my enemies, countries

32. that are powerful, and kings that are hostile to me,

33. may they subdue beneath my feet;

34. to myself and my supremacy

35. may they approach in goodness, and

36. my priesthood in the presence of ASUR and their great

37. divinities unto future days

38. may they establish like a mountain for ever.

———————

39. The power of my heroism, the might

40. of my battle, the subjection of enemies,

41. even the foes of ASUR, whom ANU and RIMMON

42. have given for a spoil,

43. on my monuments and my cylinder

44. have I described; in the temple of ANU and RIMMON

45. the great gods my lords

46. I have deposited (them) for days to come;

47. the monumental-stones of Samas-Rimmon,

48. my (fore)father I have anointed with oil; ₁ a victim

49. I have sacrificed: to their place I have restored (them).

_____

50. In future days, in the days to come,

51. at any time whatever, may a future prince,

52. when the temple of ANU and RIMMON the great

53. gods, my lords, and these towers

54. shall grow old and

55. shall decay, renew their ruins;

56. my monumental-stones and my cylinder

57. may he anoint with oil; a victim may he sacrifice;

58. to their place may he restore (them),

59. and may he write his name along with mine.

60. Like myself may ANU and RIMMON

61. the great gods in goodness of heart

62. and the acquisition of power kindly conduct him!

_____

63. Whoever my monumental-stones and my cylinder

64. shall shatter, shall sweep away,

65. shall throw into the water,

66. shall burn with fire,

67. shall conceal in the dust; in the holy house of the god

68. (in) a place invisible shall store (them) up in fragments;

69. shall obliterate the name that is written, and

70. shall write his own name, and something

75. evil shall devise, and

72. against my monumental-stones

73. shall work injury;

———————

74. may ANU and RIMMON the great gods, my lords,

75. fiercely regard him and

76. may they curse him with a withering curse.

77. May they overthrow his kingdom;

78. may they remove the foundation of the throne of his majesty;

79. may they annihilate the fruit of his lordship;

80. may they break his weapons;

81. may they cause destruction to his army;

82. in the presence of his enemies in chains

83. may they seat him. May RIMMON with lightning

84. destructive smite his land;

85. want, hunger, famine

86. (and) corpses may he lay upon his country;

87. may he not bid him live for one day;

88. may he root out his name (and) his seed in the land!

---

89. (Written) in the month Kuzallu, ₁ the 29th day, in the eponymy

90. of Ina-ili-ya-allak the chief of the body-guard. ₂

Footnotes

118:3 The *Pate'sis*, or high-priests of Assur, preceded the kings of Assyria, of whom the first is stated to have been Bel-kapkapu. As Samas-Rimmon, the high-priest, flourished 701 years before Tiglath-Pileser, his date would be about B.C. 1830. In Babylonia the high-priests were subject to a suzerain king; it is therefore probable that the high-priests of Assur also admitted the supremacy of a supreme monarch who may have ruled in Babylonia. Bricks have been found on the site of Ur in Babylonia bearing the name of Isme-Dagon, "king of Sumer and Accad," but he must have lived at a much earlier period than Samas-Rimmon, whose Babylonian contemporary was Gul-kisar.

119:1 Another mode of spelling Nahri.

119:2 Literally "have not laid down my side at the work."

120:1 Thereby turning them into Beth-els or consecrated stones. Cf. Gen. xxviii. 18.

121:1 "Of sheep-breeding," a name of Sivan or May, according to W.A.I., v 43, 14.

121:2 Literally " the mighty men," like the *Gibborim* of the Old Testament; cf. 2 Sam. xxiii. 8. Assyrian chronology was reckoned according to the eponyms, officers who gave their name to each year of the king's reign. As the inscription of Rimmon-nirari I, who preceded Tiglath-Pileser I by about two hundred years, is dated in the eponymy of Shalman-garradu ("the god Solomon is a hero"), accurate chronology in Assyria went back to an early period.

THE ASSYRIAN STORY OF THE CREATION

Translated by the Editor

FRAGMENTS of a long epic poem, describing the creation of the world in a series of tablets or books, were discovered by Mr. George Smith among the cuneiform treasures of the British Museum which had come from the royal library of Kouyunjik or Nineveh. The tablets appear to be seven in number, and since the creation was described as consisting of a series of successive acts, it presented a curious similarity to the account of the creation recorded in the first chapter of Genesis.

The epic embodied certain of the ideas and beliefs current in Assyria and Babylonia regarding the creation of the universe. That there were other ideas and legends is evident from the existence of another story of the creation, which came originally from the library of Cutha, and differed entirely from that of the epic. The epic, as I have pointed out in my *Lectures on the Religion of the Ancient Babylonians* (p. 385), clearly belongs to a late date. The gods of the popular religion not only have their places in the universe fixed, but even the period and manner of their origin is described. The elementary spirits of the old Accadian faith have passed into the great gods of Semitic belief, and been finally resolved into mere symbolical representatives of the primordial elements of the world. Under a thin disguise of theological nomenclature, the Babylonian theory of the universe has become a philosophic materialism. The gods themselves come and go like mortal men; they are the offspring of the everlasting elements of the heaven and earth, and of that watery abyss out of which mythology had created a demon of evil, but which the philosopher knew to be the mother and source of all things. The Tiamat of the first tablet of the epic is a very different being from the Tiamat of the fourth.

I much doubt, therefore, whether the epic in its present form is older than the time of Assur-bani-pal. It sums up under a poetical garb the teachings of mythology and philosophy about the origin of things. The Babylonians had always believed that the world had been created out of water, and that the present creation had been preceded by an earlier creation, an imperfect and chaotic prototype of that which followed. This earlier creation, in fact, had been the work of chaos, and the destruction of it by the younger gods of light and order ushered in the new creation of the visible world. Light and darkness, chaos and order, are ever struggling one against the other; but the victory of light and order was assured ever since Merodach, the Sun-god, overthrew the dragon Tiamat, "the wicked serpent " as she is also called, who represented chaos and anarchy. Tiamat is the Assyrian equivalent of the Hebrew *tehôm*, "the deep," upon whose face, according to Gen. i. 2, darkness had rested before the universe was made.

The cosmological system of the first tablet found its way into the pages of a Greek writer, Damaskios, who lived in the sixth century of our era (*De Prim. Princip.* 125, p. 384, ed. Kopp). "The Babylonians," he tells us, "like the rest of the barbarians, pass over in silence the one principle of the universe, and they constitute two, Tavthê and Apasôn, making Apasôn the husband of Tavthê, and denominating her 'the mother of the gods.' And from these proceeds an only-begotten son Mumis, which, I conceive, is no other than the intelligible world proceeding from the two principles. From them also another progeny is derived, Lakhê and Lakhos; and again a third, Kissarê and Assôros, from which last three others proceed, Anos and Illinos and Aos. And of Aos and Davkê is born a son called Bêlos, who, they say, is the fabricator of the world."

Tavthê is Tiamat or Tiavat, Apasôn is *ap'su*, "the abyss," and Mumis is Mummu, who, however, is identified with Tiamat in the epic, Kissarê and Assôros being Ki-sar and An-sar, "the lower" and "the upper firmament." Lakhê and Lakhos, that is to say, Lakhmu or Lakhvu and Lakhamu or Lakhavu, must be read instead of the Dakhê and Dakhos of the manuscripts. Belos is Bel-Merodach, "the younger Bel," in contradistinction to "the older Bel" of the city of Nipur, one of whose Accadian names was Illil, the Illinos of Damaskios. It is probable that the name of Lakhamu was carried to Canaan along with those of other Babylonian gods such as Rimmon, Nebo, and Sin. At all events Lakhmi seems to be the name of a Philistine in 1 Chron. xx. 5, and Beth-lehem is best explained as "the house of Lekhem," like Beth-Dagon, "the house of Dagon," or Beth-Anoth, "the house of Anat."

Only the commencement of the first tablet (numbered K 5419) has been recovered, but the tablet was of no great length, as the larger part of the reverse appears to have been occupied by the colophon. It has been published by Mr. George Smith in the *Transactions of the Society of Biblical Archæology*, iv. 2 (1876), and by Professor Fr. Delitzsch in his *Assyrische Lesestücke* (1st edition, 1878), and has been translated by Mr. Smith in his *Chaldean Genesis*. Translations of it by Dr. Oppert, Dr. Schrader, and myself have subsequently appeared. A small fragment of the second tablet has been found by Professor Delitzsch, containing the colophon, "the second tablet (of the series beginning) 'when above.'" The third tablet was partly represented by the fragments numbered K 3473, Rm. 615. Lines 17–42 of the obverse have been published by Professor Delitzsch in his *Assyrisches Wörterbuch*, i. p. 100, and portions of the text are translated in Smith's *Chaldean Genesis*. A fragment of the fourth tablet from the Library of Kouyunjik, numbered K 3437, has been published by George Smith (*Trans. Soc. Bib. Arch.*, iv. 2), and Delitzsch (*Ass. Leses.*, pp. 82, 83), and translated by Smith, Oppert, Lenormant, and others; but nearly the whole of the text has now been recovered from a tablet brought from Babylonia by Mr. Rassam (numbered 82–9–18, 3737), and published by Mr. Budge in the *Proceedings of the Society of Biblical Archæology* for 6th December 1887. A translation of it has been given by myself in my *Lectures on the Religion of the Ancient Babylonians*, pp. 379 *seq.* (1887), which I can now improve in several particulars. The fifth tablet (K 3567) was published by Smith (*Trans. Soc. Bib. Arch.*, iv. 2), and Delitzsch (*Ass. Leses.*, p. 78), and translated by Smith, Oppert, and Lenormant. About one-third of it is lost. Of the seventh (?) tablet only three small fragments remain (345, 248, 147), published by

Delitzsch (*Ass. Leses.*, p. 79), and translated by Smith in his *Chaldean Genesis*. To the third tablet probably belongs an unpublished fragment (K 3449), describing the preparation of the bow of Merodach; an attempt at its translation will be found in Smith's *Chaldean Genesis*.

No fragments of the sixth tablet have as yet been noticed. According to Professor Delitzsch the fragment belonging to the second tablet concludes with the prayer of Merodach to capture Tiamat and avenge the gods, after Anu and Ea had already declined to undertake the task (*Assyrisches Wörterbuch*, i. p. 65). The first line of the next tablet is stated to be, "An-sar (the upper firmament) opened his mouth." From this point onwards the ends of the lines are preserved on the fragment numbered K 3473, and from line 9 onwards the beginnings of the lines on fragment K 3938. They run as follows:—

1. "An-sar opened his mouth, and

2. unto him (Merodach) he speaks the word:

3. ('O lord, I) am yearning 1 in my liver;

4. (against Tiamat) let me send thee, even thee:

5. (with the snare?) thou shalt ensnare (Tiamat), thou shalt be exalted (?)

6. ...... thy ... to thy presence.

7 ...... their divine porter.

8. ...... let them dwell in feasting.'

9. The god went (saying), let them make the wine.

10. Humbly the god has ... them; let them hear the report.

11. He has established and has fixed their ..., (saying) thus:

12. 'Do thou ... thy (word) repeat to them.

13. An-sar, moreover, ... has urged me on;

14. the law of (his) heart has made me, even me, to ponder

15. thus: 'Tiamat ... has seen us;

16. she has convened (sitkunat) an assembly, and is violently enraged.'"

Here follows the passage translated further on. The last two lines of the tablet, as we learn from a small fragment, concluded with the words, "(Merodach) ascended (from) their midst (and the great gods) determined (for him his) destiny."

It will be seen that a good deal of the poem consists of the words put into the mouth of the god Merodach, derived possibly from older lays. The first tablet or book, however, expresses the cosmological doctrines of the author's own day. It opens before the beginning of time, the expression "at that time" answering to the expression "in the beginning" of Genesis. The heavens and earth had not yet been created, and since the name was supposed to be the same as the thing named, their names had not as yet been pronounced. A watery chaos alone existed, Mummu Tiamat, "the chaos of the deep." Out of the bosom of this chaos proceeded the gods as well as the created world. First came the primæval divinities Lakhmu and Lakhamu, words of unknown meaning, and then An-sar and Ki-sar, "the upper" and "lower firmament." Last of all were born the three supreme gods of the Babylonian faith, Anu the sky-god, Bel or Illil the lord of the ghost-world, and Ea the god of the river and sea.

But before the younger gods could find a suitable habitation for themselves and their creation it was necessary to destroy "the dragon" of chaos with all her monstrous offspring. The task was undertaken by the Babylonian sun-god Merodach, the son of Ea, An-sar promising him victory, and the other gods providing for him his arms. The second tablet was occupied with an account of the preparations made to ensure the victory of light over darkness and order over anarchy.

The third tablet described the success of the god of light over the allies of Tiamat. Light was introduced into the world, and it only remained to destroy Tiamat herself. The combat is described in the fourth tablet, which takes the form of a poem in honour of Merodach, and is probably an earlier poem incorporated into his text by the author of the epic. Tiamat was slain and her allies put in bondage, while the books of destiny which had hitherto been possessed by the older race of gods were now transferred to the younger deities of the new world. The visible heaven was formed out of the skin of Tiamat, and became the outward symbol of An-sar and the habitation of Anu, Bel, and Ea, while the chaotic waters of the dragon became the law-bound sea ruled over by Ea.

The heavens having been thus made, the fifth tablet tells us how they were furnished with mansions for the sun and moon and stars, and how the heavenly bodies were bound down by fixed laws that they might regulate the calendar and determine the year. The sixth tablet probably described the creation of the earth, as well as of vegetables, birds, and fish. In the seventh tablet the creation of animals and reptiles was narrated, and doubtless also that of mankind.

It will be seen from this that in its main outlines the Assyrian epic of the creation bears a striking resemblance to the account of it given in the first chapter of Genesis. In each case the history of the creation is divided into seven successive acts; in each case the present world has been preceded by a watery chaos. In fact the self-same word is used of this chaos in both the Biblical and Assyrian accounts — *tehôm*, *Tiamat* —the only difference being that in the Assyrian story "the deep" has become a mythological personage, the mother of a chaotic brood. The order of the creation, moreover, agrees in the two accounts; first the light, then the creation of the firmament of heaven, subsequently the appointment of the celestial bodies "for signs and for seasons and for days and years," and next, the creation of beasts and "creeping things." But the two accounts also differ in some important particulars. In the Assyrian epic the earth seems not to have been made until after the appointment of the heavenly bodies, instead of before it as in Genesis, and the seventh day is a day of work instead of rest, while there is nothing corresponding to the statement of Genesis that "the Spirit of God moved upon the face of the waters." But the most important difference consists in the interpolation of the struggle between Merodach and the powers of evil, as a consequence of which light was introduced into the universe and the firmament of the heavens was formed.

It has long since been noted that the conception of this struggle stands in curious parallelism to the verses of the Apocalypse (Rev. xii. 7-9): "And there was war in heaven: Michael and his angels fought against the dragon; and the dragon fought and his angels, and prevailed not; neither was their place found any more in heaven. And the great dragon was cast out, that old serpent, called the Devil, and Satan, which deceiveth the whole world." We are also reminded of the words of Isaiah xxiv. 21, 22: "The Lord shall visit the host of the high ones that are on high, and the kings of the earth upon the earth. And they shall be gathered together, as prisoners are gathered in the pit, and shall be shut up in prison." It may be added that an Assyrian bas-relief now in the British Museum represents Tiamat with horns and claws, tail and wings.

There is no need of drawing attention to the profound difference of spiritual conception that exists between the Assyrian epic and the first chapter of Genesis. The one is mythological and polytheistic, with an introduction savouring of the later materialism of the schools; the other is sternly monotheistic. Between Bel-Merodach and the Hebrew God there is an impassable gulf.

It is unfortunate that the last lines of the epic in which the creation of man would have been recorded have not yet been recovered. A passage in one of the early magical texts of Babylonia, however, goes to show that the Babylonians believed that the woman was produced from the man, conformably to the statement in Gen. ii. 22, 23. We there read of the seven evil spirits (W.A.I., iv. I. i. 36, 37) that "the woman from the man do they bring forth."

Footnotes

127:1 *Khummulu*, from *khamalu*, "to be pitiful."

THE ASSYRIAN EPIC OF THE CREATION—FIRST TABLET OF THE STORY OF THE CREATION

OBVERSE

1. At that time the heaven above had not yet announced,

2. or the earth beneath recorded, a name;

3. the unopened ₁ deep was their generator,

4. MUMMU-TIAMAT (the chaos of the sea) was the mother of them all.

5. Their waters were embosomed as one, ₂ and

6. the corn-field ₃ was unharvested, the pasture was un-grown.

7. At that time the gods had not appeared, any of them;

8. by no name were they recorded, no destiny (had they fixed).

9. Then the (great) gods were created,

10. LAKHMU and LAKHAMU issued forth (the first),

11. until they grew up (when)

12. AN-SAR and KI-SAR were created.

13. Long were the days, extended (was the time, until)

14. the gods ANU, (BEL and EA were born),

15. AN-SAR and KI-SAR (gave them birth).

The rest of the tablet is lost.

Footnotes

133:1 Or " first-born," if we adopt Delitzsch's reading *ristu* instead of *la patû*.

133:2 This is shown to be the signification of *istenis* by S 1140, 8.

133:3 *Gipara;* see W.A.I., V. i. 48-50. *Nirba kân yusakhnapu giparu 'sippâti summukha inbu*, "the corn-god continuously caused the cornfield to grow, the papyri were gladdened with fruit;" S 799, 2. *Ana gipâri eltu erubbi* (Accadian *mi-para-ki azagga imma-dan-tutu*), "to the holy cornfield he went down." The word has nothing to do with "clouds" or "darkness."

THIRD TABLET OF THE STORY OF THE CREATION

OBVERSE

17. "The gods have marched round her, ₁ all of them;

18. up to those whom thou hast created at her side I have gone."

19. When they were *gathered* (?) beside her, TIAMAT they approached.

20. The strong one (MERODACH), the glorious, who desists not night or day,

21. the exciter to battle, was disturbed in heart.

22. Then they marshalled (their) forces; they create darkness.

23. "The mother of KHUBUR, ₂ the creatress of them all,

24. I pursued with (my) weapons unsurpassed; (then) did the great snake(s) bite. ₃

25. With my teeth sharpened unsparingly did I bite.

26. With poisoned breath like blood their bodies I filled.

27. The raging vampires ₄ I clothed with terror.

28. I lifted up the lightning-flash, on high I launched (it). ₅

29. Their messenger SAR-BABA ......

30. Their bodies were struck, but it pierced not their breasts.

31. I made ready the dragon, the mighty serpent and the godLAKHA(MA),

32. the great reptile, the deadly beast and the scorpion-man, ₁

33. the devouring ₂ reptiles, the fish-man ₁ and the gazelle-god, ₃

34. lifting up (my) weapons that spare not, fearless of battle,

35. strong through the law which (yields?) not before the foe.

36. The eleven-fold (offspring), like him (their messenger), were utterly (overthrown?).

37. Among the gods her forces

38. I humbled the god KINGU ₄ in the sight (of his consort?), the queen.

39. They who went in front before the army (I smote?),

40. lifting up (my) weapons, a snare for TI(AMAT).

Footnotes

134:1 *I'skhuru-si.*

134:2 Khubur is identified with 'Su-edin on the eastern side of the Babylonian plain in W.A.I., ii. 50, 51. Professor Delitzsch suggests that the expression *ummu Khubur* may be the origin of the name Omorôka assigned by Berôssos to Tiamat.

134:3 *Ittaqur* from *naqaru.* In Hebrew the verb is used especially of piercing the eyes.

134:4 The *usumgalli* or "solitary monsters" were fabulous beasts who were supposed to devour the corpses of the dead, and were therefore not exactly vampires which devoured the living, but corresponded rather with one of the creatures mentioned in Is. xiii. 21, 22; xxxiv. 14.

134:5 *Umtas* [*sir*].

135:1 According to the 9th tablet of the Epic of Gisdhubar, "the scorpion-men" guard the gate between "the twin mountains" through which the sun passes at its rising and setting. The fish-man was Oannes, afterwards identified with Ea, who brought wisdom and culture to Chaldæa out of the Persian Gulf.

135:2 *Dapruti* (see W.A.I., v. 16, 80) from the same root as *diparatu*, "a flame."

135:3 The gazelle-god was identified by the later mythology of Babylonia, sometimes with Ea the god of Eridu, sometimes with Bel the god of Nipur: see my *Lectures on the Religion of the Ancient Babylonians*, pp. 283 *seq.*

135:4 Kingu was the husband of Tiamat.

FOURTH TABLET OF THE STORY OF THE CREATION

OBVERSE

1. So he established for him (*i.e.* MERODACH) the shrine of the mighty;

2. *before* (?) his fathers for a kingdom did he found (it). 1

3. Yea, thou art glorious among the great gods;

4. thy destiny is unrivalled; thy gift-day 2 is (that of) ANU.

5. O MERODACH, thou art glorious among the great gods;

6. thy destiny is unrivalled; thy gift-day is (that of) ANU.

7. Since that day unchanged is thy command.

8. High and low entreat thy hand:

9. may the word that goes forth from thy mouth be established; untroubled is thy gift-day.

10. None among the gods has surpassed thy power

11. at the time when (thy hand) founded the shrine of the god of the sky. 3

12. May the place of their *gathering* (?) become thy home!

13. "O MERODACH, thou art he who avenges us;

14. we give thee the sovereignty, (we) the hosts of all the universe!

15. Thou possessest (it), and in the assembly (of the gods) mayest thou exalt thy word!

16. Never may thy weapons be broken; 4 may thine enemies tremble!

17. O lord, be gracious to the soul of him who putteth his trust in thee,

18. and destroy ₁ the soul of the god who has hold of evil."

19. Then they set in their midst his saying unique; ₂

20. to MERODACH their first-born they spake:

21. "May thy destiny, O lord, go before the god of heaven;

22. may *he confirm* (?) the destruction and creation of all that is said.

23. Set thy mouth; let it destroy his word:

24. turn, speak unto it, and let him lift up his word (again)." ₃

25. He spake and with his mouth destroyed his word;

26. he turned, he spake unto it and his word was re-created.

27. Like (the word) that issues from his mouth the gods his fathers saw it:

28. they rejoiced, they approached MERODACH the king.

29. They bestowed upon him the sceptre (and) throne and reign;

30. they gave him a weapon unsurpassed, consuming the hostile.

31. "Go" (they said), "and cut off the life of TIAMAT;

32. let the winds carry her blood to secret places."

33. The gods his fathers also hear the report of EA:

34. "A path of peace and obedience is the road I have caused (him) to take."

35. There was too the bow, as his weapon he prepared (it);

36. he made the club swing, he fixed its seat;

37. and he lifted up the sacred weapon ₄ which he bade his right hand hold.

38. The bow and the quiver he hung at his side;

39. he set the lightning before him;

40. with a glance of swiftness he filled his body.

41. He made also a snare to enclose the dragon of the sea.

42. He seized the four winds that they might not issue forth, any one of them,

43. the south wind, the north wind, the east wind (and) the west wind.

44. His hand brought the snare near the bow ₁ of his father ANU.

45. He created the evil wind, the hostile wind, the storm, the tempest,

46. the four winds, the seven winds, the whirlwind, the unending wind;

47. and he caused the winds which he had created to issue forth, the seven of them,

48. confounding the dragon TIAMAT, as they swept after him.

49. Then the lord lifted up the deluge, his mighty weapon.

50. He rode in the chariot of destiny that retreats without a rival. ₂

51. He stood firm and hung the four reins at its side.

52. (He held the weapon?) unsparing, that overfloods her panoply.

53. .... their teeth carry poison.

54. ...... they sweep away the learned.

55. ...... might and battle.

56. On the left they open their ......

57. ...... fear ......

58. With the lightning-flash and ... he crowned his head.

59. He directed also (his way), he made his path descend, and

60. humbly he set the ... before him.

61. By (his) command he kept back the …

62. His finger holds the …

63. On that day they exalted him, the gods exalted him,

64. the gods his fathers exalted him, the gods exalted him.

65. Then the lord approached; he catches TIAMAT by her waist;

66. she seeks the huge *bulk* (?) of KINGU her husband,

67. she looks also for his counsel.

68. Then the rebellious one (TIAMAT) appointed ₁ him the overthrower of the command of BEL.

69. But the gods his helpers who marched beside him

70. beheld (how MERODACH) the first-born held their yoke.

71. He laid judgment on TIAMAT (but) she turned not her neck.

72. With her hostile lip(s) she announced opposition.

73. (Then) the gods (came) to the help of the lord, sweeping after thee:

74. they gathered their (forces) together to where thou vast.

75. (And) the lord (launched) the deluge, his mighty weapon;

76. (against) TIAMAT, whom he requited, he sent it with these words:

77. "(War) on high thou hast excited.

78. (Strengthen?) thy heart and muster (thy troops) against the god(s).

79. …… their fathers beside (thee).

80. …… thou hast opposed

81. …… to (thy) husband.

82. .... *lordship* (?)

83. ....thou seekest.

REVERSE

1. (Against) the gods my fathers thou has directed thy hostility.

2. Thou harnesser of thy companions, may thy weapons reach their bodie(s).

3. Stand up, and I and thou will fight together."

4. When TIAMAT heard this,

5. she uttered her former spells, she repeated her command.

6. TIAMAT also cried out vehemently with a loud voice.

7. From its roots she strengthened (her) seat completely.

8. She recites an incantation, she casts a spell,

9. and the gods of battle demand for themselves their arms.

10. Then TIAMAT attacked MERODACH the chief prophet of the gods;

11. in combat they joined; they met in battle.

12. And the lord outspread his snare (and) enclosed her.

13. He sent before him the evil wind to seize (her) from behind.

14. And TIAMAT opened her mouth to swallow it.

15. He made the evil wind enter so that she could not close her lips.

16. The violence of the winds tortured her stomach, and

17. her heart was prostrated and her mouth was twisted.

18. He swung the club, he shattered her stomach;

19. he cut out her entrails; he overmastered (her) heart;

20. he bound her and ended her life.

21. He threw down her corpse; he stood upon it.

22. When TIAMAT who marched before (them) was conquered,

23. he dispersed her forces, her host was overthrown,

24. and the gods her allies who marched beside her

25. trembled (and) feared (and) turned their backs.

26. They escaped and saved their lives.

2 7. They clung to one another fleeing helplessly.

28. He followed them and shattered their weapons.

29. He cast his snare and they are caught in his net.

30. Knowing (?) the regions they are filled with grief.

31. They bear their sin, they are kept in bondage,

32. and the elevenfold offspring are troubled through fear.

33. The spirits as they march *perceived* (?) the glory (ofMERODACH).

34. His hand lays blindness (on their eyes).

35. At the same time their opposition (is broken) from under them;

36. and the god KINGU who had (marshalled) their (forces)

37. he bound him also along with the god of the tablets (of destiny in) his right hand.

38. And he took from him the tablets of destiny (that were) upon him.

39. With the string of the stylus he sealed (them) and held the … of the tablet.

40. From the time when he had bound (and) laid the yoke on his foes

41. he led the illustrious enemy captive like an ox,

42. he established fully the victory of AN-SAR ₁ over the foe;

43. MERODACH overcame the lamentation of (EA) the lord of the world.

44. Over the gods in bondage he strengthened his watch, and

45. TIAMAT whom he had bound he turned head backwards;

46. then the lord trampled on the underpart of TIAMAT.

47. With his club unbound he smote (her) skull;

48. he broke (it) and caused her blood to flow;

49. the north wind bore (it) away to secret places. ₂

50. Then his father (EA) beheld (and) rejoiced at the savour;

51. he caused the *spirits* (?) to bring a peace-offering to himself.

52. So the lord rested; his body he feeds.

53. He strengthens (his) *mind* (?), he forms a clever plan,

54. and he stripped her of (her) skin like a fish, according to his plan;

55. he described her likeness and (with it) overshadowed the heavens;

56. he stretched out the skin, he kept a watch,

57. he urged on her waters that were not issuing forth;

58. he lit up the sky; the sanctuary (of heaven) rejoiced, and

59. he presented himself before the deep, the seat of EA.

60. Then the lord measured (TIAMAT) the offspring of the deep;

61. the chief prophet made of her ₁ image the house of the Firmament. ₂

62. Ê-SARRA which he had created (to be) the heavens

63. the chief prophet caused ANU, BEL and EA to inhabit as their stronghold.

64. [*First line of the next tablet:*] He prepared the mansions of the great gods.

65. [COLOPHON.] One hundred and forty-six lines of the 4th tablet (of the series beginning:) "When on high unproclaimed."

66. According to the papyri of the tablet whose writing had been injured.

67. Copied for NEBO his lord by Nahid-Merodach, the son of the irrigator, for the preservation of his life

68. and the life of all his house. He wrote and placed (it) in Ê-ZIDA. ₃

Footnotes

136:1 These are the last two lines of the Third Tablet.

136:2 *'Sigar*. In W.A.I., v. I, 12, we read that the 12th of Iyyar was the *'sigar* or "festival" of the goddess Gula.

136:3 Literally "the covering of heaven" (*nalbas same*).

136:4 Literally "may they open."

137:1 Literally "pour out."

137:2 The "saying," or "Word," is regarded as having a real existence which could be created, destroyed, and re-created by Merodach. The "Word" is similarly personified in Zech. ix. 1.

137:3 We have here the same idea as in the "burden" of the Hebrew prophets, the Assyrian verb "to lift up" being *nasu*, the Hebrew *nasâ*, whence *massâ*, "a burden" or "oracle."

137:4 The *badhdhu* was the name of the weapon sacred to Merodach. From the sculptures it would appear to have been a kind of boomerang.

138:1 Here we have a curiously weakened form, *kisti* instead of *qasti*.

138:2 Or if we correct the text and read *makhri la galidta*, "that fears not a rival."

139:1 Read *ip-qid*.

141:1 The primæval god of the Firmament.

141:2 The meaning of the blood of Tiamat is shown by the two contradictory Babylonian legends of the creation which Berôssos, the Chaldean historian, has amalgamated together:—"Bêlos (Merodach) came and cut the woman (Tiamat) asunder, and of one half of her he formed the earth, and of the other half the heavens, and at the same time destroyed the animals within her (in the abyss). All this was an allegorical description of nature. For, the whole universe consisting of moisture, and animals being continually generated therein, the deity above mentioned (Bêlos) cut off his own head; upon which the other gods mixed the blood, as it gushed out, with the earth, and from thence men were formed. On this account it is that they are rational and partake of divine knowledge." Similarly, according to Philon Byblios, Phœnician cosmology declared that the blood of Uranos or Baal-samaim, when mutilated by his son Kronos near the rivers and fountains, flowed into them and fertilised the earth.

142:1 "Its" in the original.

142:2 Ê-Sarra.

142:3 Ê-Zida, "the constituted house," was the great temple of Nebo in Borsippa, now represented by the Birs-i-Nimrud. The copy of the text deposited in it by Nahid-Merodach was probably made in the Persian age.

FIFTH TABLET OF THE STORY OF THE CREATION

OBVERSE

1. He prepared the twin mansions of the great gods.

2. He fixed the stars, even the twin-stars, ₁ to correspond with them.

3. He ordained the year, appointing the signs of the Zodiac ₂over (it).

4. For each of the twelve months he fixed three stars,

5. from the day when the year issues forth to the close.

6. He founded the mansion of (the Sun-god) the god of the ferry-boat, that they might know their bonds,

7. that they might not err, that they might not go astray in any way.

8. He established the mansion of BEL and EA along with himself.

9. Moreover he opened the great gates on either side,

10. he strengthened the bolts on the left hand and on the right,

11. and in the midst of it he made a staircase.

12. He illuminated the Moon-god that he might be porter of the night,

13. and ordained for him the ending of the night that the day may be known,

14. (saying:) "Month by month, without break, keep watch in thy disk.

15. At the beginning of the month light up the night,

16. announcing thy horns that the heaven may know.

17. On the seventh day, (filling thy) disk

18. thou shalt open indeed (its) narrow contraction.

19. At that time the sun (will be) on the horizon of heaven at thy (rising).

20. Thou shalt cut off its …

21. (Thereafter) towards the path of the sun thou shalt approach.

22. (Then) the contracted size of the sun shall indeed change (?) ₁

23. … seeking its path.

24. … descend and pronounce judgment.

The rest of the obverse and the first three lines of the reverse are destroyed.

REVERSE

4. [*First line of the next tablet:*] When the assembly of the gods had heard him.

5. Fifth tablet of the (series beginning) "When on high."

6. The property of Assur-bani-pal the king of hosts, the king of Assyria.

Footnotes

143:1 *Lu-masi*, literally "the twin oxen," of which seven were reckoned.

143:2 *Mizrâta*, which is the same word as the *mazzarôth* of Job xxxviii. 32.

144:1 The mutilated condition of the tablet makes the translation of this line extremely doubtful. There may be a reference in it to the star Al-tar or Dapinu.

THE SEVENTH TABLET OF THE STORY OF THE CREATION

OBVERSE

1. At that time the gods in their assembly created (the beasts).

2. They made perfect the mighty (monsters).

3. They caused the living creatures (of the field) to come forth,

4 the cattle of the field, (the wild beasts) of the field and the creeping things (of the field).

5. (They fixed their habitations) for the living creatures (of the field).

6. They distributed ₁ (in their dwelling-places) the cattle and the creeping things of the city.

7, (They made strong) the multitude of creeping things, all the offspring (of the earth).

8. ...... in the assembly of my family.

9. ...... EA the god of the illustrious face.

10. ... the multitude of creeping things did I make strong.

11. ... the seed of LAKHAMA did I destroy.

The rest is lost.

Footnotes

145:1 *Yuzahi* (*zu*).

The Following Fragment (K 3449) Belongs to the Story of the Creation, but its Position is Uncertain

1. The snare which they had made the gods beheld.

2. They beheld also the bow, how it had been stored up.

3. The work they had wrought they lay down,

4. and ANU lifted (it) up in the assembly of the gods.

5. He kissed the bow; it …

6. and he addressed the arch of the bow, (saying) thus:

7. "The wood I stretch once ₁ and yet again.

8. The third time is the … of the star of the bow in heaven.

9. I have established also the position of …

10. Since the fates" …

. . . .

Footnotes

146:1 *Istenumma.*

THE BABYLONIAN STORY OF THE CREATION ACCORDING TO THE TRADITION OF CUTHA

TRANSLATED BY THE EDITOR

BESIDES the story of the Creation in a series of successive acts, Mr. George Smith brought to light the fragments of two tablets containing another legend of the Creation which varied very considerably from it. The tablets belonged to the library of Assurbani-pal at Nineveh, but the colophon informs us that they had been copied from older documents which came from the library of Cutha, now Tel Ibrahim, in Babylonia. The text has never been published, but a translation was given of it by Mr. Smith in his

Chaldean Genesis, and a revised version by myself in the *Records of the Past*, vol. xi. As much progress has been made in cuneiform studies during the ten years which have elapsed since the latter was published, I now give another translation of the inscription, embodying the improvements which our increased knowledge of the Assyrian language has enabled me to make.

The Cuthæan legend, it will be observed, knows nothing of a creation in successive acts. Chaos is a period when as yet writing was unknown. But the earth already existed, and was inhabited by the chaotic brood of Tiamat, imperfect first attempts, as it were, of nature, who lived in a city underground. They were destroyed, not by Merodach, the god of Babylon, but by Nergal, the patron-deity of Cutha, who is identified with Nerra, the god of pestilence, and Ner, the mythical monarch of Babylonia who reigned before the Deluge. The words of the poem are put into the mouth of Nergal, and the poem itself was written for his great temple at Cutha.

The legend of Cutha agrees better with that reported by Bêrôssos than does the legend of the Epic. In both alike we have a first creation of living beings, and these beings are of a composite nature, the offspring of Tiamat or Chaos. In both alike the whole brood is exterminated by the gods of light.

The date to which the legend in its present form may be assigned is difficult to determine. The inscription is written in Semitic only, like the other creation-tablets, and consequently cannot belong to the pre-Semitic age. It belongs, moreover, to an epoch when the unification of the deities of Babylonia had already taken place, and the circle of the great gods was complete. Ea, Istar, Zamama, Anunit, even Nebo and Samas, are all referred to in it. Possibly it may be dated in the age of Khammuragas (cir. B.C. 2350).

THE CUTHÆAN LEGEND OF THE CREATION

COLUMN I

Many lines are lost at the commencement.

2. His word (is) the command of the gods ...

3. His glancing-white instrument (is) the glancing-white instrument (of the gods).

4. (He is) lord of that which is above and that which is below, the lord of the spirits of earth,

5. who drinks turbid waters and drinks not clear waters;

6. in whose field that warrior's weapon *all that rests there* (?)

7. has captured (and) destroyed.

8. On a tablet he wrote not, he opened not (the mouth), and bodies and produce

9. he caused not to come forth in the land, and I approached him not.

10. Warriors with the body of a bird of the valley, men

11. with the faces of ravens,

12. did the great gods create.

13. In the ground the gods created his city.

14. TIAMAT gave them suck.

15. Their progeny 1 the mistress of the gods created.

16. In the midst of the mountains they grew up and became heroes and

17. increased in number.

18. Seven kings, brethren, appeared as begetters;

19. six thousand (in number were) their armies.

20. The god BA-NINI their father (was) king; their mother

21. the queen (was) MELILI;

22. their eldest brother who went before them, ME-MANGAB 1 (was) his name;

23. (their) second brother, ME-DUDU 2 (was) his name;

24. (their) third brother, [ME-MAN]PAKH (was) his name;

25. (their) fourth brother, [ME-DA]DA (was) his name;

26. (their) fifth brother, [ME-MAN]TAKH (was) his name;

27. (their) sixth brother, [ME-RU]RU 3 (was) his name;

28. (their seventh brother, ME-RARA was) his name.

. . . .

COLUMN II

Many lines are destroyed.

1. ... the evil curse ...

2. He turned his word ...

3. On a ... I arranged ...

4. On a tablet the evil curse he *wrote* (?) ...

5. In ... I urged the augurs on.

6. Seven against seven in breadth I arranged (them).

7. I set up the holy *reeds* (?).

8. I *prayed* to (?) the great gods,

9. ISTAR, ..., ZAMAMA, ANUNIT,

10. NEBO, ..., (and) SAMAS the warrior,

11. the son (of the Moon-god, the ...) of the gods my couriers.

12. ...... he did not give, and

13. thus I spake to my heart

14. saying: Verily it is I, and

15. never may I go ... beneath the dust!

16. never may I go ... the prayer.

17. May I go when the son ... my heart;

18. and may I renew the iron, may I assume the black garment. 4

19. The first year as it passed

20. one hundred and twenty thousand warriors I caused to go forth, and among them

2I. not one returned alive.

22. The second year as it passed I caused 90,000 soldiers to go forth and none returned alive.

23. The third year as it passed I caused 60,700 to go forth, and none returned.

24. They were carried away, they were smitten with sickness. I ate,

25. I lamented, 1 I rested.

26. Thus did I speak to my heart saying, "Verily it is I, and

27. (yet) what have I left to reign over?

28. I am a king who makes not his country whole,

COLUMN III

1. and a shepherd who makes not his people whole,

2. Since I have produced corpses and have left a desert." 2

3. With terror of men, 3 night, death (and) plague have I cursed it.

4. With fear, violence, destruction (and) famine

5. (I have effected) the overthrow of all that exist.

6. ...... there descended.

7. ...... (I) caused a deluge.

8. .... that deluge.

9. .... all

10. the foundations (of the earth were shaken?)

11. The gods ……

12. Thou didst command me, and …

13. and *they are created* (?) …

14. Thou protectest …

15. A memorial of drinking and …

16. in supplication to Ea …

17. holy memorial sacrifices …

18. holy laws …

19. I called the sons of the augurs …

20. seven against seven in breadth I arranged (them).

21. I placed the holy *reeds* (?) …

22. I *implored* (?) the (great) gods,

23. ISHTAR, …, (ZAMAMA, ANUNIT),

24. NEBO, … (and SAMAS the warrior)

25. the son (of the Moon-god, the … of the gods my couriers)

………

COLUMN IV

Many lines are lost.

1. With …

2. the men …

3. the city NAK 1 …

4. a city which …

5. to....

6. powerful king ...

7. the gods ...

8. my hand ...

9. Thou, O king, high priest, 2 shepherd, or any one else,

10. whom the god shall call (to) rule the kingdom,

11. this tablet I have made for thee, (this) stêlê I have inscribed for thee

12. in the city of CUTHA in the temple of SULIM; 3

I 3. in the ark 4 of NERGAL I have left it for thee.

14. Hearken to the voice 5 of this stêlê, and

15. remove it not, forget 6 it not;

16. fear not, tremble not!

17. May he establish thy seat!

18. Mayest thou achieve success 7 in thy works!

19. Build up 1 thy fortresses!

20. Fill 2 thy canals with water!

21. May thy papyri, 3 thy corn, thy silver,

22. thy goods, thy property,

23. (and) thy furniture, (all) of them

24. (be multiplied)! strengthen the ... for (thy) hands!

25 ... make perfect the stores of thine increase!

26. (As for the evil one) thou shalt cause him to go forth.

27. (As for the harmful one) thou shalt enchain him.

Footnotes

149:1 *Sasur.*

150:1 "The voice" or "thunder strikes." The Accadian proper names found in the legend indicate that although in its present form it is of Semitic origin it must be based on older pre-Semitic materials. Moreover, the expression "his name" is written in Accadian (*mu-ni*) which shows that it has been quoted from an Accadian text.

150:2 "The voice goes up and down."

150:3 "The voice creates."

150:4 *Ati lutsbat.*

151:1 *Asus.*

151:2 *Buti.*

151:3 *Salummat nisi.* This passage shows that *salummat* cannot signify "brilliance," as Jensen supposes.

152:1 Perhaps *nak* (*ru*) "foreign."

152:2 *Pate'si.*

152:3 The name of the great temple of Nergal in Cutha. For the reading see my *Lectures on the Religion of the Ancient Babylonians.*

152:4 *Papakh,* "the ark "in which the image of the god was carried, and which stood in the inner shrine or "holy of holies" (*parakku*).

152:5 Literally "mouth."

152:6 *Tensi* for *temsi.*

152:7 *Sipar.*

153:1 *Urrim,* whence *arammu,* "a wall."

153:2 *Nabli*; comp. *nubalu,* W.A.I., i. 15, vii. 57.

BABYLONIAN LAWSUITS AND JUDGMENTS

TRANSLATED BY DR. OPPERT

HAVING worked for more than five-and-twenty years at the Babylonian and Assyrian deeds of contract and legal decisions, and having explained the documents relating to these subjects which have been discovered in Mesopotamia, I am now able to state that the meaning of these difficult texts is at length fairly well understood by us. The simplest explanation is that which is the most difficult to obtain, and I have no doubt that the translations and interpretations I offer will appear to many scholars so easy and conclusive as to make them assume that any one might have discovered them at the outset. Fortunately, however, not only the translations of other scholars, but my own imperfect ones as well, have been published, and will thus convince younger students of the immense difficulty there is in arriving at results which seem so evident.

The first texts which I have selected contain certain contracts and legal decisions relating indubitably to captive Jews who had been carried to Babylon after the destruction of Jerusalem. One of the most interesting of them is a lawsuit commenced by a Jewish slave named Barachiel in order to recover his original status. A copy of the text has been published by Father Strassmaier in the *Transactions of the Oriental Congress* at Leyden, No. 42.

My translation of it, which will appear in the *Transactions of the Oriental Congress* at Vienna, has been amended in one or two points. The translations offered by Dr. V. Revillout and a young Assyriologist, Dr. Peiser, are very imperfect, Dr. Revillout having entirely misunderstood the nature of the suit referred to, and having fallen into several grammatical errors, while Dr. Peiser's rendering is not less unacceptable.

The case was as follows:—Barachiel, who bears the same name as the father of Elihu in the Book of Job (xxxii. 2, 6), had been the property of a wealthy person named Akhi-nuri, who had sold him to a widow of the name of Gagâ, about 570 B.C. He remained in the house of this lady as a slave, with the power of liberating himself by paying a sum equal to his *peculium*, or private property which he had been allowed to acquire, like a slave in ancient Rome; but it seems that he was never fortunate enough to be able to afford the sum of money required. He remained with Gaga twenty-one years, and was considered the *res* or property of the house, and as such was handed over in pledge, was restored, and finally became the dowry of Nubtâ ("Bee"), the daughter of Gaga. Nubtâ gave him to her son and husband in exchange for a house and some slaves. After the death of the two ladies he was sold to the wealthy publican Itti-Marduk-baladh, from whose house he escaped twice. Taken the second time, he instituted an action in order that he might be recognised as a free-born citizen, of the family of Bel-rimanni; and to prove that he was of noble origin he pretended that he had performed the matrimonial solemnities at the marriage of his master's daughter Qudasu with a certain Samas-mudammiq. ₁ Such a performance, doubtless, implied that the officiating priest was of free birth, and that no slave or freedman was qualified to take part in it. He declared, "I am a *mar-banî*," or "descendant of a *banû* ₂," literally a "generator," or "ancestor," one of those semi-mythical heroes who gave their names to the noble families of Babylon. ₂ "I belong," he went on to say, "to the family of Bel-rimanni," who in other texts is called a high-priest. The case was brought before a court of justice, and the royal judges asked Barachiel to prove that he was of free birth. This *actio prœjudicialis de ingenuitate* was urged for and against, and eventually Barachiel was obliged to retract his former statements. He was unable to rebut the evidence alleged against him, and though it is probable that the two married persons whose "hands he had joined" were dead, other witnesses came forward who proved that he was a slave with the power of purchasing his freedom.

The exact date at which the judgment was delivered is not quite certain, but it must be later than the seventh year of Nabonidus, when the father Itti-Marduk-baladh was still alive.

I will now proceed to make some further remarks on the details of the case, as it is very interesting, and offers some useful hints as to the legal procedure of the Babylonians.

The name of Bariki-ili or Barachiel is evidently that of a Jew. He is called "a slave of ransom," that is to say, not a slave who has already purchased his freedom, since in that case he would have been free, but a slave who was allowed by special laws to employ his private fortune in the work of liberating himself. He professes to have been the *avil taslisu* or "joiner" of the hands of bride and bridegroom at a wedding which must have taken place before the thirty-fifth year of Nebuchadnezzar's reign, when he still belonged to the house of Akhi-nuri, "the seller of the slave," as he is called at the end of the text.

After the declaration of the slave, the document is comparatively easy to understand. The judges, after perusing all the evidence, do not find any proofs that Barachiel was a man of free birth, and accordingly say to him: "Prove to us that you are the descendant of a (noble) ancestor." Thereupon Barachiel confesses that he is not free-born, but has twice run away from the house of his master; as, however, the act was seen by many people he was afraid, and said, "I, am the son of a (noble) ancestor."

"But I am not free-born," he continues, and then gives an account of the events of his life.

The words *mar-banut* in line 16 signify "condition of being a free-born citizen," and not "letter of clientship," as Dr. Peiser supposes. The expression "letter of citizenship" (*dippi mar-banut*) occurs several times, and signifies the warrant given by a master to his emancipated slave. "Non-citizenship" was the fourth fact guaranteed by the seller of a slave to the purchaser, the other three being: (1) that the slave should not rebel or run away; if he returned to his former master he was to be sent back; (2) that no claim should lie against the validity of the sale on account of technical or other errors; and (3) that the purchaser should be secured against any claim made upon the services of a slave by a royal officer.

Barachiel adds that after the death of the two ladies Gaga and Nubtâ, he was sold for money to Itti-Marduk-baladh, of the Egibi family, thus becoming a *servos redimendus argento*, a slave who could be ransomed with money, and that he awaits the sentence of the court.

The judges decided that Barachiel should be restored to his original status, and added that it was in the *uzuz* (or *usuz*) of the two married persons Samas-mudammiq and Qudasu that the judgment was pronounced. This may signify "absence," the two having died during the interval of more than twenty years which had elapsed since the marriage. It is probable that Barachiel had invented the story of his taking part in the wedding because he thought that its falsity could not be detected. If, however, the word is equivalent to the expression *ina du-zu*, the texts from Sippara would go to show that it must mean "in the presence of."

It may be remarked that not a word is said about "a deed of slavery," which was certainly not given to a slave in order to prove his own servile condition as a *vindex libertatis*, as Dr. Revillout seems to imagine.

The only penalty imposed upon the slave is his restoration to his ancient condition; penalties were decreed against those who wished to annul a contract, not against those who pretended to be free citizens. In this respect the Babylonian law was more humane than the Roman. This is the more surprising, since it cannot be denied that severe penalties were at times inflicted. The Micheaux-stones, for example, inscribed in the twelfth century before our era, threaten the transgressors of a contract and those who annul their covenants with the curses of the gods, each of whom would inflict a special punishment. The old Jew escaped with the failure of his attempt to recover his undeserved loss of liberty; perhaps the court took into serious consideration his fidelity to his former master, who had esteemed him to be worth not only a house but other slaves as well.

TRANSLATION OF A BABYLONIAN LAWSUIT RELATING TO A JEW

1. Barachiel is a slave of ransom ₁ belonging to Gagâ the daughter of

2. ...... whom in the 35th year of Nebuchadnezzar, king of BABYLON, ₂

3. [from Akhi-]nuri, the son of Nabu-nadin-akh, for the third of a mina and 8 shekels

4. she had bought. Recently ₃ he has instituted an action, saying thus: I am the son of a (noble) ancestor, of the family ₄ of Bel-rimanni,

5. who have joined the hands (in matrimony) of Samas-mudammiq the son of Nabu-nadin-akh

6. and the woman Qusadu the daughter of Akhi-nuri, even I. In the presence of

7. the high-priest, ₅ the nobles and the judges of Nabonidus king of BABYLON

8. they pleaded the case and listened to their arguments in regard to the obligation of servitude

9. of Barachiel. From the 35th year of Nebuchadnezzar king of BABYLON

10. to the 7th year of Nabonidus king of BABYLON, ₆ he had been sold for money, had been put

11. in pledge, (and) as the dowry of Nubtâ the daughter

12. of Gagâ had been given. Afterwards Nubtâ had alienated him by a sealed contract;
₇

13. in exchange for a house and slaves to Zamama-nadin

14. her son and Idinâ her husband had given him. They read (the evidence) and

15. said thus to Barachiel: Thou hast brought an action and said: The son of a (noble) ancestor

16. am I. Prove to us thy (noble) ancestry. Barachiel his former statement

17. retracted, saying: Twice have I run away from the house of my master, but many people (were present),

18. and ₁ I was seen. I was afraid and said (accordingly) that I am the son of a (noble) ancestor.

19. My citizenship exists not; I am the slave of ransom of Gaga.

20. Nubtâ her daughter received me as (her) dowry; Nubtâ

21. alienated me by a sealed contract, and to Zamama-nadin her son and Idinâ ₂ her husband

22. gave me in exchange; and after the death of Gagâ (and) Nubtâ,

23. to Itti-Marduk-baladh the son of Nabu-akhe-iddin of the family of Egibi, for silver

24. I [was sold]. I am a slave. Go now, [pronounce sentence] about me.

25. [The high-priest], the nobles and the judges heard the evidence

26. [and] restored [Barachiel] to his condition as slave of ransom, notwithstanding the absence of Samas-mudammiq

27. [the son of Nabu-nadin-akh] and Qudasu the daughter of Akhi-nuri, the seller ₃

28. [of the slave]. For the registration of this [decision] Musezib the [priest]

29. [and] Nergal-akhe-iddin the judges

30 of the family of Epis-el, in the city of the palace of the king of BABYLON, the 17th day of

31. the month Marchesvan ₁ [the 7th? year] of Nabonidus king of BABYLON.

Footnotes

156:1 The father of Akhi-nuri was Nabu-nadin-akh ("Nebo gives a brother"), and the father of the son-in-law bears the same name. But it is by no means certain that the uncle married his niece, since the two persons may have been different.

156:2 It would be a useful work to collect the names of all the *banû* or ancestors, men of noble birth, like Egibi, Nur-Sin, and others.

160:1 For the meaning of this expression see above, p. 158.

160:2 B.C. 590.

160:3 *Ana eninni*, not a proper name as Dr. Revillout supposes!

160:4 Read *lu zir*. Several distinguished persons were called Bel-rimanni, among others a priest of the Sun-god.

160:5 *Sangu.*

160:6 B.C. 549.

160:7 The text does not seem to me to have been correctly copied here.

161:1 Not *ka*.

161:2 Such names are all, I think, emphatic imperatives: Idinâ, "give!" Basâ, "exist!" Iribâ, "multiply!" Considering the Aramaic transcription of the last name, we ought perhaps to pronounce Idinai, Basai.

161:3 *Nadinan*, a singular noun with the same termination as *makhiranu*, "the buyer;" *masikhanu*, "the measurer;" *paqiranu*, "the plaintiff;" *napalkattanu*, "the defendant."

162:1 October.

INSCRIPTION OF MENUAS, KING OF ARARAT, IN THE VANNIC LANGUAGE

TRANSLATED BY THE EDITOR

SINCE the publication of my Memoir on "The Cuneiform Inscriptions of Van Deciphered and Translated " in the *Journal of the Royal Asiatic Society*, xiv. 4, 1882, we have begun to learn something about a race of kings who ruled on the shores of Lake Van in Armenia, from the ninth to the seventh centuries before our era. The founder of the dynasty, Sarduris I, the son of Lutipris, who reigned in B.C. 833, introduced the cuneiform system of writing as well as other elements of Assyrian culture into the country over which he was king. The inscriptions he has left us are in the Assyrian language; but his successors discontinued the use of a foreign tongue, and the language of their texts is invariably their native one. It is semi-flectional in character, and possibly belongs to the same family of speech as that of which Georgian is the modern representative. For want of a better name it is known as Vannic. The story of its decipherment will be found in the Memoir above cited.

The grandson of Sarduris I was Menuas, a prince who carried his arms far and wide, and has bequeathed to us numerous records of his wars and buildings. Far away from his capital of Dhuspas or Tosp, near the mountain of Rowandiz and the Lake of Urumiyeh, on the summit of the pass of Keli-shin, 12,000 feet above the level of the sea, is a monument of his campaigns, which is wrapt during the greater part of the year in a coating of ice; in the north he engraved his inscriptions beside the banks of the Araxes, while the record of his campaign against "the land of the Hittites" is inscribed on the cliff of the Euphrates at Palu, about midway between Malatiyeh and Van.

The inscription translated here was copied by Schulz and Sir A. H. Layard from a stone built into the wall of a vault under the church of Sts. Peter and Paul at Van, and a squeeze of it has been taken by Captain Clayton. The transliterated text and analysis will be found in my Memoir, xxxii. p. 555. The text is mutilated in parts, and at the time my Memoir was published I was unable to restore some of the passages in it. The progress that has since been made, however, in the study of the Vannic inscriptions, enables me now to supply their deficiencies, and also to correct and supplement the translation I then gave. For the sake of Vannic scholars I append here a transliterated text of the inscription as it should read after the restoration of the missing characters:—

1. [*god* Khal-di-]ni-ni us-ma-si-ni *man* Me-nu-a-s *man* Is-pu-u-i-ni-[khi-ni-s]

2. [a-li-e] i-u tu-su-kha-a-ni *land* Ma-a-na-a-i-di us-ta-a-di

3. [*land* e-ba-]a-ni-a tu-u-bi a-ma-as-tu-u-bi i-ku-u-ka-a-ni

4. [sali si-su-kha-ni-]e *person* Khu-ra-di-ni-li *plural* kid-da-nu-u-li kha-a-i-tu-u

5. [*man* Sa-da-ha-li-]e-khi-ni-ni *land* -ni-ni *city* Su-ri-si-li-ni *city* Tar-khi-ga-ma-a-ni

6. [*city* ...]-dhu-ra-a-ni *man* Sa-da-ha-li-e-khi-ni-da-a-ni ap-ti-ni

7. [*city* ...]-li-e-i *stone* gar-bi-e *land* Kha-ti-na-as-ta-a-ni ap-ti-ni

8. ...... i u-e *land* Al-zi-i-ni-ni IIMCXIII *person* ta-ar-su-a-ni

9. [sa-li-]e a-li-ke za-as-gu-u-bi a-li-ke *alive* a-gu-u-bi

10. [*god* Khal-di-]e a-li-ma-a-nu a-ru-u-bi *person* Khu-ra-di-na-u-e *plural* We learn from the inscription that the land of the *Khate* or Hittites extended as far north as Alzi, the situation of which is given in the inscription of Tiglath-Pileser I (i. 64; see above,

p. 94, note 4), and that Sada-hadas, whose name was perhaps pronounced Sanda-hadas, was the king of that portion of the Hittite nation with which Menuas was brought into contact. The mention of the name of the Khate or Hittites on this and other Vannic monuments shows that the name was not confined to the Hittites of the south.

INSCRIPTION OF THE VANNIC KING MENUAS

1. (To the KHALDIS-gods), 1 the gracious, Menuas the son of Ispuinis 2

2. (speaks) thus: In the spring (?), when I had approached the land of MINNI 3

3. I carried away the people of (that distant country), I partitioned (them). The same

4. (year), after collecting the (baggage) of the army, the fruits (?) 4

5. of the country of the son of Sada-halis, the cities of SURISILIS, TARKHI-GAMAS, 5

6. (and) ... DHURAS, which is called the seat of the son of Sada-halis,

7. the stones of (the city of) ... lis, which is called the seat of the HITTITES,

8. (I captured), and 2113 soldiers of (the year), 1 belonging to the country of ALZIS,

9. partly I killed, partly I took alive.

10. (To KHALDIS) I brought all and each of those who belonged to the army.

Footnotes

166:1 The supreme god of Van was Khaldis, but as each tribe or district also worshipped a god of the same name, there were many Khaldis-gods who are invoked by the Vannic kings along with the supreme Khaldis of Van. It was from the worship of Khaldis that the population of a part of Armenia became known to the Greeks as Khaldæi, a name naturally confounded with that of the Chaldeans of Babylonia.

166:2 The Vannic kings usually call themselves kings of Biainas or Bianas, a name which has passed through the Byana of Ptolemy into the modern Van. Van is now, however, the name of the city which the Vannic kings called Dhuspas or Tosp, instead of denoting a district as it did in their time, Tosp being now the name of the district. Biainas was known to the Assyrians under the name of Urardhu, the Ararat of the Old Testament. Mount Ararat, it may be noted, is a modern designation, the name of

Ararat not being applied to the country north of the Araxes in the Biblical age, and "the mountains of Ararat" of Genesis viii. 4 signifying, as in the Assyrian inscriptions, the Kurdish mountains to the south of Lake Van.

166:3 The Mâna of the Vannic texts are the Mannâ of the Assyrians, the Minni of the Old Testament, whose position is shown by the inscriptions to have been immediately to the west of the kingdom of Van, from which they were separated by the Kotûr range.

166:4 *Khai-tû* may be connected with *khai-di-a-ni*, "fruits" (from *khai*, "to grow"), but it may also be a compound of *tu* and *kha*, "to possess," like *'sui-du*, "to set for a possession," or *abili-du*, "to set on fire."

166:5 Tarkhi-gamas seems to be compounded with the name of the Hittite god Tarkhu, like Tarkhu-lara, king of the Gamgumâ, and Tarkhu-nazi, king of Malatiyeh, mentioned on the Assyrian monuments.

167:1 This expression is of frequent occurrence in the Vannic texts, and its literal translation is certified by ideographs; but what it means is doubtful.

THE ANCIENT HEBREW INSCRIPTION OF SILOAM

TRANSLATED BY THE EDITOR

THE oldest Hebrew inscription yet discovered is engraved on the rocky wall of the subterranean channel which conveys the water of the Virgin's Spring at Jerusalem into the Pool of Siloam. The history of its discovery is curious. In the summer of 1880 one of the native pupils of Dr. Schick, a German architect long resident in Jerusalem, was playing with some other lads in the Pool, and while wading up the subterranean channel slipped and fell into the water. On rising to the surface, he noticed, in spite of the darkness, what looked like letters on the rock which formed the southern wall of the channel. Dr. Schick, on being told of them, visited the spot, and found that an ancient inscription, concealed for the most part by the water, actually existed there.

The first thing to be done was to lower the level of the water, so as to expose the inscription to view. But his efforts to copy the text were not successful. He was not a palæographer; and as the letters of the inscription, as well as every crack and flaw in the stone, had been filled by the water with a deposit of lime, it was impossible for him to distinguish between characters and accidental markings on the rock, or to make out the exact forms of the letters. The first intelligible copy was accordingly made by myself during my visit to Jerusalem in February 1881. As, however, I had to sit for hours in the mud and water, working by the dim light of a candle, my copy required correction in several points, and it was not until the arrival of Dr. Guthe six weeks later that an exact facsimile was obtained. Dr. Guthe removed the deposit of lime by the application of an acid, and so revealed the original appearance of the tablet. A cast of it was taken, and squeezes made from the cast which could be studied at leisure and in a good light.

The inscription is engraved on the lower part of an artificial tablet cut in the wall of rock about 19 feet from the place where the subterranean conduit opens out upon the Pool of Siloam, and on the right hand side of one who enters it. The conduit is at first about 16 feet high; but the height gradually lessens until in one place it is not quite 2 feet above the floor of the passage. According to Captain Conder's measurements, the tunnel is 1708 yards in length from the point where it leaves the Spring of the Virgin to the point where it enters the Pool of Siloam. It does not run, however, in a straight line, and towards the centre there are two *culs de sac*, the origin of which is explained by the inscription. We there learn that the workmen began the conduit simultaneously at both ends, like the engineers of the Mont Cénis tunnel, intending to meet in the middle. But they did not succeed in doing so, though the two excavations had approached one another sufficiently near for the workmen in the one to hear the sound of the pickaxes used by the workmen in the other. How such a feat of engineering was possible in the age when the tunnel was excavated it is difficult to understand, more especially when we remember that the channel slopes downward through the rock, and winds very considerably. It may be added that the floor of the conduit has been rounded to allow the water to pass through it more easily.

The Pool of Siloam is of comparatively modern construction, but it encloses the remains of a much older reservoir. It is situated on the south-eastern extremity of the hill, sometimes, but erroneously, called Ophel, which lies to the south of the Temple-hill, now represented by the Mosque of Omar, but separated from the latter by the remains of a valley, which was first perceived by Dr. Guthe and Dr. Schick. The Virgin's Spring is on the opposite side of the hill, but more to the north, overlooking the valley of the Kidron. As it is the only natural spring, or "gihon," as the Jews would have called it, in the neighbourhood of Jerusalem, the command of its supply of water was of primary importance to the inhabitants of the Jewish capital. It was, however, outside the walls of the city, and hence the necessity of cutting a conduit through the hill which should convey its water to a reservoir within the town. We are told in 2 Chron. xxxii. 4 that when the Assyrians invaded Judah Hezekiah "stopped all the fountains," that is to say, he concealed them under masonry or earth. The Virgin's Spring or Gihon must have been similarly sealed up, while its water was conducted into the city through a subterranean channel.

The date of the inscription has occasioned a good deal of controversy, some scholars assigning it to the reign of Hezekiah, and others to an earlier period. The chief reason for believing it to have been a work of Hezekiah is that in 2 Kings xx. 20 it is stated that "he made a pool and a conduit, and brought water into the city," while in 2 Chron. xxxii. 30 we read that he "stopped the upper watercourse of Gihon, and brought it straight down to the west side of the city of David." But a more literal rendering of the latter passage would be, "he stopped the exit (*môtsa*) of the waters of the Upper Gihon, and he directed them downwards on the west side of the city of David." Here it is evident that by the Upper Gihon is meant the Spring of the Virgin, for which the word *môtsa* or "exit" is employed in the inscription. Besides the Upper Gihon there must have been another or Lower Gihon, which can have been none other than the Pool of Siloam. This had become a second source of water-supply, and might therefore with propriety be named "a spring."

It would consequently appear from the chronicler's words that the Pool of Siloam already existed in the time of Hezekiah, and that what the Jewish monarch did was to excavate a second conduit, running from the Pool, not in a winding direction like the tunnel of Siloam, but in a straight direction along the western side of the city of David. Now such a conduit has actually been discovered cut in the rock and leading from the Pool of Siloam to another reservoir which once existed below.

There is, moreover, evidence in the Book of Isaiah that the tunnel of Siloam was in existence before Hezekiah came to the throne. In Isaiah viii. 6 a prophecy is recorded, uttered while Ahaz was still reigning, in which allusion is made to "the waters of Shiloah that go softly." This can hardly refer to anything else than the gently-flowing stream which still runs through the tunnel of Siloam. The inference is supported by the name Shiloah itself, which probably signifies "the tunnel," and would have been given to the locality in consequence of the channel which was here excavated through the rock.

The characters of the inscription exhibit to us the alphabet which was used by the prophets before the Exile. They belong to what may be termed the southern or Jewish branch of the old Phœnician alphabet, a parallel branch to which was used in Moab, and is found on the Moabite Stone. The forms of some of the letters are more archaic than those on the Moabite Stone, the forms of others less so. Similar forms are met with on early Israelitish and Jewish seals, which go back to a period preceding the Captivity. They are characterised by a peculiarity which shows not only that writing was common, but also that the usual writing material was papyrus or parchment, and not stone or metal. The "tails" attached to certain letters are not straight as on the Moabite Stone or in Phœnician inscriptions, but rounded. The words, it may be added, do not always end with the line.

The language of the inscription is the purest Hebrew. It presents us with only one unknown word, *zadah* in line 3, which seems to mean "excess" or "obstacle." Why it should have been engraved on the lower part of a carefully-prepared tablet, where the water of the conduit would necessarily conceal it, it is impossible to conjecture. The upper part of the tablet may perhaps have been intended to contain a royal inscription giving the name of the king under whom the work was executed.

One fact, however, is made very clear by the text. Whether it were the Siloam tunnel itself, or the second tunnel leading from it to a lower reservoir, that was constructed by Hezekiah, in either case the Pool of Siloam would lie "on the west side of the city of David." "The city of David" must, accordingly, have stood on the southern hill, the so-called Ophel; and since the city of David was identical with Zion, according to 2 Samuel v. 7, this hill must represent the original mount of Zion. Consequently the valley of the Sons of Hinnom must be the valley which was known in the time of Josephus as the Tyropœon or Cheesemakers'. It once divided both the Temple hill and the southern hill from the mountains on the west, though it is now choked with the rubbish which the numerous destroyers of Jerusalem have thrown into it. In some places the rubbish is more than 70 feet deep, and under it, if anywhere, we must look for the tombs of the kings that were cut in the rocky cliff of the city of David. Here, too, if anywhere, will be found the relics of the temple and palace that Nebuchadnezzar destroyed, overlaid with the accumulations of more than two thousand years.

A cast of the Siloam inscription may be seen in the rooms of the Palestine Exploration Fund, and facsimiles in Canon Isaac Taylor's *History of the Alphabet*, i. p. 234, and in *Fresh Light from the Monuments*, p. 101.

1. (Behold the) excavation! Now this is the history of the excavation. While the excavators were still lifting up

2. the pick, ₁ each towards his neighbour, and while there were yet three cubits to (excavate, there was heard) the voice of one man

3. calling to his neighbour, for there was an *excess* (?) in the rock on the right hand (and on the left?). And after that on the day

4. of excavating the excavators had struck pick against pick, one against another,

5. the waters flowed from the spring ₁ to the pool ₂ for a distance of 1200 cubits. And (part) ₃

6. of a cubit was the height of the rock over the head of the excavators.

END OF VOL. I

Printed by R. & R. CLARK, *Edinburgh.*

Footnotes

174:1 *Garzen*, translated "ax" in 1 Kings vi. 7, where it is used of the instrument with which the stones of Solomon's temple were quarried.

175:1 *Môtsâ*, literally "exit," which is used of the Upper Gihon or Virgin's Spring in 2 Chron. xxxii. 30.

175:2 *Berêchah*, rendered "pool" in 2 Sam. ii. 13, Isaiah xxii. 9, 11, etc. We learn from the latter passage (Isaiah xxii. 9, 11) that there were at least three "pools" or reservoirs in Jerusalem in the time of Hezekiah, and yet our inscription shows that there must have been a period when only one such reservoir existed, since it terms the Pool of Siloam "the pool."

175:3 A flaw in the rock makes this word doubtful. It begins with m and ends with t, and appears to consist of three letters.

Made in the USA
Coppell, TX
11 January 2022

71422080R10094